Walk Gently

Upon the Earth

Walk Gently Upon the Earth

Linda Hogan

Published by Lulu.com ~ http://www.lulu.com

Printed in the United States of America.

The examples within this text are factual, to the best of the author's knowledge, based on candid discussions with persons interviewed during the research and writing of this book or the personal experience of the author. The names, places, and details of the situations have been changed to protect the privacy of the persons to whom the events occurred.

Any brand and product names mentioned herein are trademarks or registered trademarks of their respective owners.

ISBN 978-0-557-17600-7

Table of Contents

Dedication

I dedicate this book to

Mother Earth

and

all mothers . . . those who love, nurture, and protect

And in loving memory of my beautiful mother,

A. Jennette Creamer,

who taught me the value of wildness

Acknowledgments

Many special people and places have made this work possible by supporting me emotionally and physically. I am eternally grateful.

I thank, first, my two wonderful children, Will and Molly, who love and accept me for who I am. I thank them for the great patience they displayed at having a mother who spent more time playing in the woods than cleaning the house and whose idea of decorating usually involved stones, feathers, bones, and weeds. I thank them for not openly showing their embarrassment of having a mother who was known as a Wild Woman. They are the loves of my life. I am grateful to my ex-husband, Bill, who has always been my friend and supported me in my need to follow my own path.

The journal entries, which have now become this book, were first e-mail messages to my dear friend Roland Comtois, who never tired of listening to my tales of encounters with frogs, dragonflies, or trees. Without his never-ending encouragement and belief in me, this book would not have come to print. I am indebted to him also for sharing his daughter, Kaitlin, with me, after my own daughter was too old to play in the woods, and for allowing me to fill her head with magic and her room with fairy dust. I appreciate Tim Morvan, my favorite chef, who shared so much more than comfort food with me when I was tired and needy.

My friends Dianne Pepin and Cat Yelle, my true soul sisters, shared so many adventures with me. Always seeing from the heart and looking with wonder at the world and God's creations, they taught me that every day is a blessing.

Betsy and Sam Harding, thank you for your friendship and sharing your beautiful home in the New Hampshire woods with me and for the companionship of Carter, my favorite pooch. Lucy Gatchell and Dexter Harding, you are true stewards of the Earth. I have been so honored to stay in your cabin in the field of wildflowers and feast from your organic garden. It was the perfect spot to finish up my book.

All of those mentioned and many more have inspired me to write, but without the help of the following two people my book would have stayed in my computer and never come to print. Ann Martelle, my Earth-connected friend and a copywriter, volunteered to edit the manuscript for me. She taught me that you don't capitalize every word you like. Ann is someone I can trust to be totally honest and when she said she liked the book, I knew I needed to get this out for others to read. John Catlin, you truly must be an Earth Angel. You listened to my computer woes, told me not to worry and from the goodness of your heart took over and turned a messed up manuscript into a book that I'm proud of. I thank you from the bottom of my heart.

Prologue

Oh Great and Holy Spirit,

I take this step into the day you have given.

I embrace all that I see,

the season, the wind, the fragrances, the weather.

Let me always accept the day given with a grateful heart.

Today I shall walk in love and be your humble servant.

Native American prayer

Stories, Messages, and Meditations

Introduction

Each morning when I step outside my door I walk into the Garden of Eden. "O Great Spirit, thank you for this beautiful day."

There has not been one day in the past 20 years that I have not started my day this way and really meant it. When you are truly connected to Mother Earth and Spirit, you see as much beauty in a cold, gray, sleety, December morning as a warm, sunny day in June.

It reaffirms that Spirit is with me each day no matter what circumstances face me. This has gotten me through the deaths of my father and mother, heart-wrenching incidents with my children, and the ending of my marriage. It gives me strength to face whatever the day may bring. Being in nature has helped to open my eyes to the beauty that is right in front of me.

Oh, what a gift I've been given. Since a little girl, I have felt more at home outdoors than in any house. The woods and fields have been my home since I could remember, with wild creatures my family and friends.

I have loved everything to do with the natural world my whole life. I was labeled a tomboy early on, which gave me tremendous freedom. I was allowed to play in the woods and dirt. Muddy hands, skinned knees and torn pants were accepted as my attire and I grew healthy and happy.

It wasn't until the seventh grade, when some of my friends were becoming interested in the opposite sex that I was made aware that girls dressed and acted differently than boys. I gave up sneakers and playing in the mud for penny loafers and talking on the phone.

When my own children were born, my love of the outdoors was once again rekindled. I felt like that eight-year-old girl again, sharing with them the secrets I had learned so long ago about spiders, dandelions, grasshoppers, and the smell of the Earth after a spring rain. I taught them to find salamanders under rotting logs and guided them not to touch them with their warm little hands. I explained that being cold blooded, hot fingers would feel like sticks from a fire to the little salamanders, and it was best to just watch and talk to them from a small distance. What a joy to share what I loved most with those I loved most.

As my children grew up, developed interests of their own, and moved away, I still took time to play in the woods. I knew the woods intimately and celebrated the birth of each jack-in-the-pulpit, fern, and wildflower.

Although I have always felt a connection to nature, I first recognized that I was on a spiritual journey 20 years ago when I was asked to teach Native American art and culture at a children's camp. My job was to share stories and teach Native American crafts to 200 children each day. I accepted the position and was assigned an activity area in the woods.

As I spent time setting up my area in the woods, I started to feel a connection to the past and started to research early Native American life and spirituality. The values of love, respect, and sharing resonated with me and I began to look at life and my connection to the Earth more seriously. If I wanted to teach and share those values with children, I would have to live those values myself.

I was struck by the fact that Native American tradition is to recognize Spirit in everything. I started to look at the natural world a little differently. I spent many hours that summer in the woods teaching what I was learning from my native friends to the children in my charge. My days got longer and longer as I arrived hours before the children and stayed in the woods well after they had left for the day. It was this quiet time alone in the woods that started to awaken me. I felt at peace and very protected in the woods.

I marveled at the changes taking place in my life. I had boundless energy and found myself transforming into a different person. It was noticeable to those around me that I was no longer the sweet, quiet, always-pleasing woman they had known. There was a strength and power growing inside me that was hard for some to accept. I was becoming the woman I was meant to be—and that woman spoke up for what she believed in and had a very strong will and sense of truth. This caused some distress to my family as they adjusted to this stranger who had taken my place. It was time for us all to learn independence and it temporarily made for a very uncomfortable family situation. Years later, my children have shared how they respect and appreciate me for making the decision to follow my own path.

My path leads through the woods, fields, and swamps. It nourishes me so that I may go out into the world and attempt to make a difference in the lives of others. My business and life as I know it now are a direct result of spending time in nature and learning to "just *be*."

I once saw nature as most people do. They are looking through foggy glasses and don't even know it. Preoccupied with what they perceive as life's trials and tribulations, feeling that they're running out of time and never getting ahead, they seek happiness in their work and the material things that it can provide. The happiness from these material gains fades quickly and they work harder to buy the next toy or bauble to bring back the elation. Running like hamsters on a wheel they speed by the very miracles and gifts that will finally bring them peace and happiness.

A few weeks ago, I pulled to the side of the road during rush hour to watch a glorious sunset colored turquoise, purple, and coral pink reflect over a small pond. It was there for less than five minutes and it faded into darkness. It saddened me to watch others, minds preoccupied with what to fix for dinner or mulling over the aggravations of the day, speed by and miss this magical and soul-nourishing sight. I've encountered runners with headphones speeding along on wooded paths, oblivious to the symphony of birds. The gifts of the Earth are so precious and they are free.

Mother Earth puts on a constant show and never charges admission. What I now see is incredible. I know that, as I continue to be in nature, I will be gifted with more and more sight.

We were once wild and one with the Earth. Some of us were fortunate enough to start off our lives running wild through woods and meadows; others of us spent our childhood in the city and may not feel the same connection. It is never too late to make this connection to the Earth. It is what sustains and energizes us but most no longer remember. We are moving so quickly in today's world that our experiences are blurred. We need to slow down so that our senses will awaken and our hearts will open. When we learn this and reconnect to nature we are able to receive her energy and the many gifts she has for us.

Yesterday, as I walked across my newly mowed lawn, I looked down to see tiny white flowers. I took the time to get down on my hands and knees to look at them. They were exquisite little pansy-like flowers with blue faces. Beside them, so tiny that they were invisible to anyone standing, were perfect little blue star-shaped flowers with a yellow center. What a gift. Had I not been down on the ground I would never have seen them.

Take a few minutes once in a while to survey the world at your feet. It is marvelous and beautiful and inspiring. Why were these little plants, virtually invisible to the naked eye and small enough to be spared by the mower, created so perfectly? I believe it is because everything is food for our soul. They are there for those of us who take the time to connect to Mother Earth and once our eyes have been opened we see no end to the beauty around us.

I have been receiving gifts from nature and the universe for many years now. These are tangible gifts that others can see. They are there if you slow down and choose to look. I have seen rainbows in a clear sky. I've enjoyed the company of a mourning dove who chose to build her nest each year at the entryway to my back door. We were eye-to-eye and greeted each other each time I went in and out. She stayed long after her babies had flown away. I've had a prairie grow up on a small plot of land in my New England backyard with rare and unusual plants. Beautiful blue morning glories miraculously bloomed at my back door on my birthday, planted by birds or fairies or God. The frost on the window of my meditation room is like none I have ever seen. There are perfect ferns, feathers, and messages. I've also received gifts of Native American objects that I believe to be from my spirit guides.

The natural world is God's gift to us. It is the easiest, but often the most neglected, way to connect to Spirit. It takes no preparation. There is no chanting or visualization involved. You need only sit. Sit and *be*. Listen to the voice of Mother Nature and open your eyes to what is in front of you. Do not think—merely observe and listen.

If you were to commit yourself to sitting outside in a peaceful, quiet spot for a short time every day for a week, you would start to notice incredible changes taking place in your life. First you would notice your attitude. Any depression or anger naturally lessens as peace and happiness takes its place. Mother Earth freely shares her energy with you and you will find yourself walking with a lighter step and with a feeling of physical well-being.

Your creativity starts to flow and problems seem to dissipate as new ideas come into being. Your vision starts to clear and all of a sudden you find yourself marveling at colors and patterns you never knew existed. You stop to listen to the music of nature and it fills you with incredible love. "Yes!" you shout as you remember. "This is who I *am!*"

I am *Love*, and I am living in the Garden of Eden.

May this book be a peaceful respite for you in a fast-paced, sometimes chaotic world. Page by page, may your eyes be opened to the glory of Gaia, allowing her to lead you back to your own personal Garden of Eden.

A Message From Mother Earth to Her Children

Channeled through Linda Hogan on June 19, 2008

Wake up children . . . Wake up now.

Weren't you taught that it is not good to harm those who take care of you?

I have been here in the past and I will be here in the future to take care of you.

Find a sanctuary, a place of peace where you can go and think of ways to help me instead of harm me.

Encourage others to do the same.

Sitting with me, you will receive my energy, which will help you stay peaceful and calm. Do not go out into the world unless you are peaceful and calm. Take the time to ground yourself with my energy before going out. Do not add to the confusion; add to the peace.

The energy coming into the planet at this time is very strong. It flows and ebbs and flows again, and those of you who are sensitive are happy one moment and anxious or sad the next, and then euphoric, and an hour later depressed or angry. You may question if you are going crazy and, at the very least, think you're in a state of depression. Be patient and know you are not alone.

The fact that you are feeling this way only serves to help you recognize that you are becoming more sensitive to my energies and those of the universe. It is good and will serve you well in the future. Be patient with those others who feel these energies and react to them because they do not have the resources that you do.

Remember: we are all *one*.

Looking Through the Eyes
of a Child

Remember to slow down and smell the crayons.
Cat Yelle

This winter morning I sit in my chair by the window sipping coffee, inhaling the aroma and watching the steam swirl like a mini tornado. Looking out, I see a huge yellow butterfly—or is it a fairy dancing by the old fence post? It sparkles after all; it must be a fairy. I sit here letting my imagination take me to a wondrous place.

In reality, it is a yellow plastic bag that has been caught on a bush. Each time the wind blows, the bag flies up and into my vision. I could sit here thinking about going out to put it in the trash where it belongs, or I could fill myself with negative energy thinking how careless someone has been to let it escape to fly into my yard. Instead, I choose to see through the eyes of a child and see the magic in the moment. This mini-vacation to magical lands will set the tone for my entire day.

Walking on city streets, I rejoice and celebrate when I see the bright yellow head of a dandelion or the sky blue flowers of a tenacious chicory plant that has forced its way with determination through a tiny crack in the sidewalk. I was totally amazed this summer by the five foot tall thistle plant that grew up from the edge of a storm drain in the next city block. I was even more amazed and delighted that it was left there by the neighbors to thrive and bloom; I appreciated the fact the neighbors left it alone, instead of plucking it out as a weed.

I try to breathe life in deeply wherever I go. Once, walking past a junkyard with a friend, I was stopped by the scent of a rose.

"What are you doing?" she asks. "Let's just get out of here. It stinks and it's dirty."

"No, it doesn't stink. It smells like roses. You are making a judgment and not actually experiencing what is real. Now open your eyes and look. Find the rose among the trash," I commanded.

She rolls her eyes at me, but gazes into the junkyard. "There it is, between the rusty old school bus and the Volkswagen! I've found it!" she squeals like a child. "It's pink and it's beautiful and I can smell it."

There is beauty to be found everywhere if we'll only open our senses and see. If we search hard, we can find beauty in almost any situation. When you learn not to prejudge and look for the beauty, usually even the ugliest circumstance is redeemed.

Letting my imagination run wild for awhile, I become a child again. My creativity blooms and my soul dances.

Mystical Morning

As the light of the sun embraces the creatures of the Earth, so my love
nurtures myself and others.
Laura Stamps, "LOVE" from *Songs of Power*

Sharing yesterday's adventure with my dear friend Steve (like myself, a child of the Earth), I hear the excitement in his voice as he says, "You have to go back today. You must!"

"Yes," I agree. "I will go back." But I have my doubts that anything out of the ordinary will happen today. Yesterday was incredible, but to expect more would be . . . ludicrous. I roll the word around in my mind, thinking how it is much more pleasant than the word "ridiculous." I'm brought back to the present by Steve who is calling my friend Mary to the phone, insisting that I tell *her* the story, too. As I hear myself begin the retelling of yesterday's events, it seems even more like a fairy tale . . .

"Yesterday, Mary," I began, "I got up early and, looking out from my kitchen window, saw dew sparkling on the lady's mantle planted on the far side of the yard. I love how it captures the moisture in the air and turns it into little jewels that reflect everything around them. It was a beautiful morning and a slight haze lingered over the horse corral . . . and there, next to it, was the path into the pine woods inviting me to enter and breathe the cool, fragrant air. You know how I love the smell of damp and decay . . . just like you. We're such fairies."

Once on the path, there was no turning back. I sighed, thinking of scrambled eggs and coffee cooling on the counter. The woods were damp and dew was turning spider webs into sun catchers that I longed to take home and put in my windows. I scanned the woods for the wild honeysuckle giving off its spicy fragrance as sunbeams touched it. Ah, lady slippers have come and gone and now bushes and trees are adding their touches of color to this late spring woods. It was quite a mystical morning, fog lifting over the pond and the woods sparkling. Ahead on the path, I saw what appeared to be a glowing tree.

"Don't tell me," Mary interrupted. "You've been chosen as the next Moses."

"No, better than that," I tell her. "Just listen."

As I near the "burning bush," I see that it is a dead branch from a tree, without bark, smooth and shining silver in the sun. I feel the smoothness of it as I walk past and head down the path to the cornfield. A moment later, I hear the message, "Get the stick." Not wanting to carry the stick with me, I ignored the voice. The message repeated, "Get the stick."

"But I don't want to carry the stick to the cornfield and back again," I told myself.

"Get the stick," I heard again. So, you know how it is: I yanked the stick out of the ground and set off down the path. It did make a rather good walking stick.

I reached the cornfield and walked around the edge to the old grinding stone where I sit and meditate. I sat there in the hollow of the stone, my new walking stick propped in front of me, and stared out at the bright green field of new corn. Lost in a blissful state watching yellow and white butterflies play in the wildflowers at the edge of the field in front of me, I paid little attention to the bird that was chattering behind me. All of a sudden, I felt a push on my back and then more insistent chatter and then another push.

"Show yourself," I thought. A feisty tufted titmouse landed on the tip of my walking stick. She insistently called to me again—although I did not hear in words what she said. I agreed to her unknown request and said, "Yes, go ahead."

In a second, she had transferred from the branch to the top of my head where she proceeded to pull out six strands of hair, then flew off. A little laugh escaped from me as I realized what she'd asked.

Did this really happen? I was questioning myself, when once again I heard the chatter. This time, without waiting for my consent, she flew to exactly the same spot upon my head and began to pull. Six strands of hair again. As she flew away I burst out laughing, unable to control the glee I felt. What incredible magic.

"Steve thinks I should go back again today," I tell her. "I can't imagine it will happen again, do you?"

"No," my friend answers, "but you'll never know unless you do. Call us later."

This time I finish my breakfast before heading to the woods. I'm curious, but not expecting anything to happen, find my spot at the edge of the field in the grinding stone which fits my bottom perfectly. I connect to the Earth and sit just being, soaking up the late spring day.

Ten minutes pass and without warning, or permission, she lands and immediately starts to gather my hair. She makes two trips to the trees with my curly golden hair and weaves it into her nest. I never saw her again. Nor did I find her nest later in the season after her babies had flown away. Oh, what a treasure *that* would have been. Oh, what a treasure that experience was.

I believe myself to be the richest woman alive.

Omens in the Sky

Each day comes bearing its gifts. Untie the ribbons.
Ann Ruth Schabader

"Wake up, Dianne," I whispered as my friend answered her phone at five o'clock one morning. "I'm supposed to go to the beach this morning and I don't have a clue why."

Do you have a friend like that? One you can call any time of day or night with a request, no matter how silly? A soul sister who turns you into a fairy on your 50th birthday with garlands of flowers and a flimsy little violet dress, and feeds you mangos while you sit on a carpet of soft green moss in the woods and reads to you a story she has written for just this occasion. Ahh, how blessed am I to have a fairy friend, a playmate to romp in the woods with me whenever I call.

Dianne, muffins and coffee in hand, met me at my house and I started driving to our favorite rocky beach about 20 minutes away. We sat silently while driving through the backwoods roads to the highway, our bodies not quite awake, sun filtering through the trees as it started to rise above the horizon. We reached the highway, sipped on our coffee, and finished waking up.

"Why is it we're going to the beach so early?" Dianne quizzed me with a slight whine in her voice.

"I don't know yet, but you know it'll be an adventure. It always is," I replied.

We rode in silence for a few more minutes when I saw it. "Dianne, look at the sun. There is a rainbow around it; do you think it has anything to do with being called to the beach?"

"I think that's a 'sun dog.' Don't you remember Grandfather Oak telling us to watch the sky for signs that the old ways will once again be coming back?" she said. "He told us not everyone will see them, only those truly connected to the Earth."

We kept our eyes on it as we traveled to the ocean, waiting for it to disappear. Sometimes, in the blink of an eye, they can be gone—but it had been fifteen minutes since we first spotted this one. We parked the truck and clambered over the rocky beach to a field of stones polished smooth by the tumbling of ocean waves. Lying back on the stones, they seemed to turn to marshmallows under our backs as we relaxed into them.

This had been our favorite form of relaxation and rejuvenation for many years. We'd lie on our backs and ask the stones to take away any negativity, pain or frustration. We always left feeling renewed and ready to face whatever life wanted to hand us.

Today, we just laid back and relaxed and stared at the wonder before us—and then the magic happened. Before our eyes, another rainbow in the form of a chevron appeared below the rainbow-haloed sun. Staring in amazement we whispered to each other as if our voices would make it disappear. In awe, our hearts split wide open as we watched this V flatten out into a horizontal rainbow and move from below the "sun dog" to the right until it was out of sight. Soon after, the sun lost its rainbow halo and we silently made our way back to the truck. Sipping the remains of our cold coffee, we'd look at each other once in awhile and just shake our heads.

"It must have been there. We both saw it," we chimed in together. That made us laugh.

Back on the highway, and almost home, we were approaching a stand of tall pine trees on the left when we witnessed a dense grey cloud of mist come from the trees across the road to completely engulf our truck. The windows were open and it passed through the cab and over us and went into the woods on the other side of the road. I pulled the truck over and we sat there trying to make sense of what had just happened.

"Are we in some weird hallucination together?" I asked.

"Yes, I think we are." Dianne answered. "How do you feel?"

I thought for a moment and could only describe it as euphoric.

"I feel the same," Dianne said. "Maybe it was a giant puff of weed or maybe one or both of us is dreaming this fantastic dream."

Whatever it was, dream, hallucination, initiation, or signs from above, we knew without a doubt that we had truly been blessed.

Grandpa's Rainbow

Love comforteth like sunshine after rain.
William Shakespeare

My son, Will, and his cousins were very close to their grandfather. My dad had worked hard all of his life, doing what he thought was the best for his family. As little girls, my sister and I didn't get to spend nearly enough time with him.

It was a blessing that illness in his later years slowed my father down; our children spent many happy days hanging out with Grandpa. Now that our children are grown, they have let it slip out at family gatherings that it wasn't just storytelling with Grandpa. It seems that Grandpa, whom we entrusted with the care of our "little boys," had them driving him to the corner store to pick up cigars when they were eight.

My Dad loved cigars and races. There was a dog track in our city and, because Dad was diabetic and legally blind, we'd let the boys go with him to make sure he got around without getting hurt. Being naïve, my sister and I believed Dad when he said he just liked to sit and watch the races. Sit he did, because early on, he'd taught the boys how to place bets.

I shudder to think of it. For one thing, you would never bring a child to a place like a racetrack now. We perceived the world as safer then, and I believe it was. My sister and I never gave it a thought. We knew it was a bunch of other old men like my Dad just looking for an afternoon away from home. We cringe now when we think of it, but Grandpa and his boys all had a wonderful time, and we picked them up each time happy and unharmed.

As the boys grew older, Grandpa grew sicker. After many months in the hospital, he died. The boys, not yet teenagers, were very saddened by their Grandfather's death and did the best their best to cope.

After the funeral we returned to the family home, grown-ups in one room and children playing outside. Chris, the oldest grandchild, came in and asked if the boys could walk down the street to the little store to get root beer. We gave them some money and watched them cross the street listlessly. They came back twenty minutes later joking and smiling. Something had lightened their load a little, but we were too wrapped up in our own grief to question them.

Several weeks later while Grandma was watching them, they shared how they had gone to the store, got their root beer and, as they walked home, a huge rainbow appeared in the sky in front of them. It was a clear sunny day, and they knew it was Grandpa coming to say a special good-bye just to them and to let them know he was alright.

Whenever they see a rainbow, they will always remember the adventures and the love that was shared with their grandfather.

I have kept my eyes on the sky as Grandfather Oak, a Huron elder and my dear friend, told me. I have been blessed to see many rainbows. I once saw a perpendicular rainbow, shining like a pillar of color over the sacred cornfield behind my house. Another time I saw a rainbow stretch between two clouds and I have seen many sun dogs and sun halos.

There are scientific reasons for all of these; however, I notice that I see them when I need them most, when I'm sad or frustrated being a child of this Earth. To me, they are a sign of great love.

The Quickening

There is a vitality, a life-force, an energy, a quickening, that is translated through you into action, and because there is only one of you in all time, this expression is unique.
Martha Graham

The heat is almost oppressive on this hot August afternoon, but I've found a peaceful place to rest under the young green pines in the grove by the brook. The pine needles are warm and soft under my body as I stretch out on my back and gaze up through their branches, picking out stars and other familiar shapes formed by the intertwining of branches.

What a lovely occupation for a lazy afternoon. I close my eyes and tiny sparrows come to peer down and call to me. They know me from many years of sharing their woods. I believe they remember the day I caught one of their babies as it was tossed out of a nest by what could only have been a teenage member of some squirrel gang.

Walking through the woods, I heard a commotion of bird calls and screeches and followed them. Just as I reached the tree, a tiny bird came falling through the air. Instinctively reaching my hand out, it fell perfectly into my palm. We were both shocked. I gently set it in a fork of branches near the trunk and quietly slipped away to watch as the mother bird came to stay with her young one, perhaps with the hopes of teaching it how to fly back into its nest. That was early in the spring, but I trust that they still remember.

My work done for the day, I now lay back in a lazy, dreamy stupor enjoying this sultry summer day from the shade of the pines. Is the movement I'm feeling part of a dream? I open my eyes and just lie there feeling a gentle wave beneath my body. It subsides and I think it must be my imagination, and then there it is again. I question whether it is an earthquake, but know that it is much too smooth and gentle, and an earthquake in New England is rare. It reminds me of the gentle wave of life you feel when you put your hand on the stomach of a pregnant woman.

My mind searches for answers. Only when I finally give up trying and just lie back and experience it, I hear Mother Earth say, "Do not be frightened. This is a glorious time of rebirth. However, as with any birth, there is trauma to the mother and child. In order for the children to be nurtured, the mother must stay strong. With your conscious connection to the Earth and channeling of love to me, you will help me stay strong and aide me in transmuting the energies of *fear*. I, in return, will continue to give you everything you need to thrive in all ways."

How blessed and honored we are to assist in and witness this new birth of the human spirit.

Tell Them

A Channeled Message From My Mother

I AM the Great Mother.

I AM the Archangel of the Earth.

I AM reaching out to you, calling out to you.

I need you and long to connect with you.

I love you unconditionally;
although you continue, in your ignorance,
to hurt me.

I AM here to comfort you and rejoice with you.

You and I are one.

I have become a neglected part of you.

I wish to heal you so that you may heal and protect me.

Tell them.

Summer Solstice in a Sacred Cornfield

Many men walk by day, few by night. This is a delicious evening, when the whole body is one sense and imbibes delight through every pore. I go and come with a strange liberty in nature, a part of herself . . .
Henry David Thoreau

We had been anticipating this evening for a long time and headed down the woods path to the cornfield at dusk. Dianne walked ahead carrying her flute, a blanket, and strawberries fresh from the garden. I walked behind her laden with candles, a box of matches, my rattle, fairy dust, and purple goblets to hold sweet raspberry liquor our friend Cat had made. It was the summer solstice and we were there to celebrate the beginning of summer on the longest day of the year.

While day turned to dusk, we said our intentions to the universe and Dianne played her flute while I rattled. We toasted Mother Earth and shared the wine and strawberries with her. Then we sat silently on the Earth in the middle of a sacred cornfield, once home to Wampanoag Indians so many years before. We listened as birds sang the evening to sleep, and the woods were silent except for the frogs chanting in the nearby swamp.

I reached for a match and lit sage to honor the Earth, our ancestors, and the spirits that guarded this land. I reached for another match to light the candle, but the box was empty. Not worried, we just agreed that most likely we weren't supposed to have light.

We sat peacefully in meditation. Soon there appeared a glowing mist rising half way up the trees lining the edge of the field. We watched as the sky above the trees started to glow a soft red. Dianne poked me to make sure she wasn't imagining it and I squeezed her hand to assure her that yes, once again we had most likely slipped into another dimension.

Because of our connection to Mother Earth, our eyes and senses have been opened beyond what most humans experience. It was incredibly powerful and after several hours we reluctantly said good-bye and thanked Mother Earth. We packed up our belongings and headed for the edge of the field. It was 10:30 PM and we realized finding the path without light would be difficult. Peering into the night, we found the path and entered the dark woods. We stood for a moment, gaining courage to follow the narrow path of rocks and roots back the quarter mile to my yard.

With our first steps, the path ahead of us began to glow. We looked for the moon overhead, but it was a cloudy and moonless night. Continuing on our way, we saw the ferns beside the path glowing, too. I looked at Dianne and saw that we, too, were giving off a golden light, which illuminated our path ahead. We reached the yard and parted silently keeping the sacredness of the solstice close to us.

What a beautiful message to receive on such a magical night. If you have the courage to strike out into the unknown darkness with trust and follow your heart, your soul will illuminate your path.

Thank you, Spirit, for the blessings of this night.

Gaia

As I stir from sleep, I hear her softly calling my name.
Come. Come. Be with me today.
I quietly dress and silently slip out the door.

I hear her in the distance and I follow.
I can now smell her subtle perfume, and breathe in the closeness of her,
as I follow down the path.

Every once in a while, I feel her teasing caress as she circles around me,
beckoning me to join her,
to move forward on the path.

Closer to her now, I feel the heat rise from her body
as I smell her musky, intoxicating breath
on this summer day.

I am one with her once again.
She surrounds me with her spirit and brings me home.

Making Love to a Tree

No tree grows by itself. Trees are surrounded by other trees, plants, insects, animals and birds. A whole community surrounds a tree. If you lose the tree, you lose the community.
a Hopi elder

Hug a tree? Oh, no, you want me to hug a tree? I don't think so. What can I get out of hugging a tree? Someone might see me.

This was the reaction I got today when I asked the group known as Outdoor Women to hug a tree. A Wild Woman from upstate New York invited me to their yearly gathering to share my knowledge of the Earth. These rough and ready, independent women were great with a gun or fly rod, but they had a lot of hesitation about embracing a tree. I knew they would thank me later, and they did.

"If you feel self-conscious," I told them, "I suggest you find a tree off the beaten path to start. Find a place where you'll be comfortable enough to place all your attention on the tree and what you are feeling."

Find a tree that you're drawn to and just go up and put your arms around it, like you're hugging a dear friend.

Place your ear against the tree while you're embracing it and listen.

Once you've relaxed and let go of your fear that someone may see you, the experience can begin.

What you hear while your ear is pressed up against the trunk of the tree is the life force or sap flowing through its veins. It is easier to hear the life within the tree in the spring than it is in winter, but as you tune yourself into nature more and more each day, your senses will open and you will be able to feel the pulse of life deep within a winter tree.

Initially when hugging the tree you'll feel how it sways and moves gently. After more practice, you will start to discern the energy being sent to you from the tree.

Different types of trees give off different types of energy. Pines are very generous with their loving energy and it is an excellent one to start with. Oak trees, as you might imagine, have a more supportive energy. There is a grove of beech trees that I visit where I often lie down on the Earth in the center of their circle. I find their energy happy and uplifting. It feels very nurturing, like being in a circle of caring friends.

When you find a tree that draws you back again and again, it is time to formally ask that it send you energy. Tell it that you are grateful and will receive it willingly.

Embracing the tree, open your heart to it and receive the energy. If you are sad or depressed or physically or mentally tired, tell the tree. Share your needs and feelings with it and it will do its best to send you the kind of energy you need. Often, when I pour out my troubles to the tree, it will respond with advice that generally is very helpful. I have been doing this for so long that I have clear communication with the trees I sit with regularly. I've felt loved, appreciated, and sometimes sexually aroused. Whatever energy came through it was exactly what I needed to renew my spirit and body. Soon you will be in communication with the trees and plants, and you will feel their excitement and appreciation that you are among them.

If you live in the city and don't have access to deep woods, you will do well to go to a local park and find a tree to sit under and lean against. Just close your eyes and rest against the tree. Allow yourself to connect to the Earth where you sit. Just relax your body against the trunk of the tree. You'll soon feel a hug of energy surrounding you. Use your imagination to feel the embrace of the tree and enjoy the energy that is being offered to you. When you are ready to leave the tree you've been sharing time with, remember to thank it for sharing its healing energy with you. Thank it for sharing its lessons on how to give shelter and support, how to take and receive nourishment and how to bow and bend.

When first starting this exercise you may need to use your imagination to feel the embrace of the tree. That is perfectly fine. Your conscious mind is feeling self-conscious or having trouble believing what is not yet remembered. Have no doubt that your ancestors long, long ago were connected to the plant world and enjoying and using their energy. The more times you do this exercise the easier it will become and the more rewarding it will be.

A very sad occasion for me was leaving my beautiful woods to move to the city. I had lovingly visited and cared for the 80 acres of woods behind my house for seventeen years.

On my first exploration of the land around the house I'd live in for many years to come, I appointed myself steward of the forest, field, and ponds—land which was undeveloped and owned by a big Boston real estate trust. Several times it was threatened with development; each time I and the neighbors abutting the land formed a committee to fight the developers. Twice we were successful, but it was an ongoing battle . . . one which I would now have to leave to the others. I went one last time to sit under the tree by the brook where I had been meditating for many years. I shared with the tree my grief about leaving and it sent its energy around me for one last time. Very clearly I heard in my heart the message, "Do not weep, for when you sit under any other tree, you sit with me for we are all one." It was comforting, and it was true. For when I sit with other trees, in any other part of the world, although their energy may feel different, I always feel deeply and unconditionally loved.

Now . . . will you go hug a tree?

By the way, it turned out to be a wonderful day for the Wild Women I asked to hug a tree. I heard giggles and tears come from the woods. Only two out of twenty walked away shaking their heads.

Advice From a Tree

Stand tall

Sink your roots into the Earth

Be content with your natural beauty

Go out on a limb

Drink plenty of water

Remember your roots

Enjoy the view

– author unknown

Trees breathe in what we exhale and we breathe in what the trees exhale. We were made for each other.

Message in the Mist

A flock of geese . . .
Now in the dark flying low over the pond . . .
I stood in the doorway and could hear their wings.
Henry David Thoreau

The fog and falling leaves are calling me this morning, so I hastily pull on my favorite old jeans and t-shirt. Not bothering to run a comb through my hair I run outside.

It is like stepping into the other world. Little fairy houses and spider webs sparkle in trees as I make my way down the path. Dark pines and the yellow-green of the beech glistening with morning jewels is my gift for awakening with the birds on this fine morning.

I walk to the edge of the cornfield and step eagerly into the mist, trees barely visible on the other side. It is now that I hear the sound, a deep rumbling . . . like a train coming into a station.

As I stand silently, listening intently, out of the mist comes a large flock of Canadian geese, their wings whirring them to a stop. They let out a cry of greeting as they land all around me. Ahh, I breathe it all in, give my thanks and enjoy the beautiful moment. I feel a little sad knowing I am the only witness to this magical scene. I turn to my canine companion. "Okay, Katrina, let's get back, I've got work to do."

A message comes loud and clear through the fog. "This is your work! You and so few others see my beauty. You are keeping me alive. It is a noble work that you do. If there was no one to appreciate the gifts I offer, I would have no reason to exist. If you were never appreciated, you would surely fade and die. I am the same. The job you have chosen is an important one. This you must never doubt."

Back in my office, I am feeling very mellow. Now I will start in on the work for which I will be paid in cash—but knowing the real rewards, the priceless jewels I'm adorned with, are found out in nature communing with Mother Earth.

When Fear Comes to Sit in Your Lap

Love is grabbing hold of the Great Lion's mane and wrestling and
rolling deep into existence.
Hafiz, *I Heard God Laughing*

Cuddled in the energy of my favorite tree, a swamp maple growing beside the brook, and lost somewhere outside of time, I don't feel the intruder come near. I only feel the loving embrace of the tree and Mother Earth as they so generously fill me with their energy, something I've been lacking lately. Often when your life is filled with helping others, you neglect to take care of yourself. It has been a busy week, but I've made time today to go to the woods to replenish my soul.

My own energy has blended with Mother Earth now and I'm part of the universe. It is an incredible feeling . . . a feeling of truly being home and being loved. Now that my parents have both passed and my children have lives of their own, I sometimes get the feeling of belonging nowhere. But today I am home and in my favorite spot with sun streaming through the trees as I listen to the song the brook has for me today.

Satiated and content I'm ready to go back out into the world. I open my eyes and look with appreciation at the beauty around me.

Everything is so much clearer and more beautiful after I've made my Earth connection. Slowly I look around and my eyes are drawn to my lap. For a moment I stare in disbelief, and then gasp for air as the panic sets in. Here I am face to face with one of my greatest fears.

Here, curled up in the crease of my jeans is a tiny little garter snake. I know they are not dangerous, but I've always feared snakes and my initial reaction is to scream, jump up and run away. Instead, thanks to the energy of peace and compassion that Mother Earth has so generously shared with me, I am able to consciously look at this tiny creature who feels so comfortable in my lap.

I make peace with this tiny being as I stroke him noting that he is not slimy at all, as I had imagined snakes to be, but feels like warm leather. I gently remove him from my pants and he curls around my finger before I set him down in the leaves. As he slithers off, I vow to be more understanding of his larger brethren.

What did I conclude from this encounter? Perhaps some of my other fears are unfounded. When I take a moment—or more—to look at them honestly from a place of peace and compassion . . . I can then choose how I wish to respond.

And, if I don't want snakes to curl up in my lap, I have no business meditating on the ground in the sun.

A Time That Shall Not Be Forgotten

September 11, 2001

What a world in distress. It is incomprehensible. The world as we knew it may never be the same. My mind is trying to wrap itself around what has happened and what the future may hold.

Little did I know the signs being shown to me yesterday were a warning of things to come.

My friend Patt and I traveled to New Bedford, as we do every week, to gather up the Mayan immigrants who wish to learn English and American culture. Sometimes we go to a restaurant or store so they can practice the skills we've taught them, but yesterday I had an incredible headache. It felt as if my head was forcefully being pushed down into my body. I tried to shake it off. Patt also complained of discomfort in her shoulders so we decided to pick up our students and take them to the classroom where we'd initially taught them. Usually these young men, who work in the fish processing plants, are eager to learn. They had found their way to New Bedford and the fish industry to work hard and raise money to support their families back in Guatemala. Once farmers, their land had been seized by the government and turned over to Pepsi Cola, an American company. A huge bottling plant had taken the place of their farms and homes. They no longer could support their families. Rather than watch their wives, children and mothers starve, they made the dangerous journey to the United States, hoping to make enough money to keep their loved ones alive and save enough to return to their beloved land one day.

Today the usually happy and sociable men were distracted and quiet. We asked if anything was bothering them and they looked uncomfortable, but said no. We ended class and drove them back to the drop-off point. As soon as the car stopped, the doors flew open and they scattered in different directions.

"What on earth is going on?" Patt asked me.

I had no answer for her. Usually when we ended our rides together there would be hugs and farewells and plans made for the following week's class. This was unsettling and very unusual. We drove home to relax and get rid of our own aches and pains before going off to see clients at our healing centers.

The pressure in my head lasted all night and then suddenly, late in the morning, it left as quickly as it had come. I was on my way home from a networking meeting when my friend and associate Roland called.

"Are you on your way to work?" he asked.

I replied that I was. Our offices were next door to each other, and I told him to tell anyone looking for me that I'd be a little late.

"Linda", he said, "turn on the radio right now. I have to go. I'll see you when you get here."

I pressed the play button and caught the words "has been hit." Within seconds I heard the news that a plane had crashed into one of the Twin Towers in New York in what they believed to be a terrorist attack. Like everyone else that day I was stunned, numb, and frightened by what I heard.

When I arrived at work, my friend met me at the door and said, "Let's go get some lunch. It's going to be a long day and it will help ground us."

During lunch, I started to feel a strange pull on my abdomen and belly. It was as if the entire lower half of my body was being pulled out of my body and into the ground. Supporting me, Roland and I left our lunches and made our way back to our offices. As a spiritual counselor and well-known medium, Roland was being called by many to be consoled. He also was feeling the pain and confusion of those passing in New York. I had no explanation for the pain and discomfort I was feeling and went to lie down.

It was then that Mother Earth spoke to me.

"Thank you my dear. I'm sorry for the discomfort that you feel, but I have needed to call upon the energy of all of you who are a part of me. I am using your energy to help transmute the pain and anger and fear that is so present at this moment. I could not do it on my own because my energy has become so depleted. Stay strong and know that you are helping and the discomfort will not last."

I relaxed, it all made sense now, and several hours later the sensation had left. I was honored to help in this way.

September 12, 2001

Two days until the Wild Women Weekend. I had been planning this event for over six months, and forty-three women had made reservations and paid for the retreat I'd organized in the Connecticut woods at a wonderful old camp. It was to be a weekend of rejuvenation and learning. Spirit had much more in store for us than even I could imagine.

The calls started coming in late last night.

"The weekend has been cancelled, hasn't it?" they queried one after another.

"*No*, it hasn't," was my response. "For some reason, Spirit has called us all to be together at this time. It will be okay. Don't worry, we're meant to do this," I reassured them. I was still exhausted from my experience the afternoon before with Mother Earth and wondered what really lay ahead for all of us. Spirit was urging me forward and I had to trust what I was feeling.

September 14, 2001

Forty women, all of them nervous, some leaving children behind, finished packing and headed for the Connecticut woods. Women who had never met each other or me trusted their hearts and followed Spirit's calling.

We drove from all directions through streets lined with people holding candles to show solidarity of a country now threatened in a way we never believed possible. It was a sight both beautiful and frightening, and many arrived with tears in their eyes. These strong, beautiful wild women hugged and supported each other as they made their way to the lodge where we'd be spending the next couple of days.

I requested that they call their loved ones and give them the phone number of the office because I was asking them to turn off their cell phones while here. If there were any emergencies, the office would take the call. I also requested that televisions and radios be taken out of the bunk houses and buildings we'd be in. The owners of the camp would monitor the news and if anything major came up, we'd be notified. The women, although not quite sure, agreed.

September 15, 2001

Basically, the weekend had gone along as planned. "Planned" is a loose term, because I've learned in the past that my only real job here is sending out invitations. Spirit tends to take over in mysterious and always interesting ways.

When it came time for the group circle that evening, the women shared how inexplicably they had felt compelled to come to the retreat although most of their family members were unhappy about it and pleaded with them to stay home. Two of the women had never left their young families, and another woman married twenty years had never spent a night away from her husband, but here they were deep in the Connecticut woods with a bunch of strangers.

I welcomed them and passed a talking stick to the next in the circle. The talking stick was a wonderful invention passed down by Native Americans—probably women—who knew that each member of the community had input that was valuable, but also that we as humans get so excited that we interrupt with more to add, whereupon everything gets out of control and it turns into a wild rumpus. The talking stick is a remedy to that phenomenon.

I had brought along some CDs by Karen Drucker, a songstress that all Wild Women love. I'd carefully programmed my little player with the perfect songs in the order I thought best. Each woman would take a turn and pass the talking stick, and I'd hit the button to play one of the chosen songs. Instead the player would skip to another, more perfect song that related to what had just been said. It happened every time, and randomly Spirit picked out whatever songs were most appropriate. What a wonderful way to lighten up the serious conversations!

During these daily, end-of-day gatherings the women reiterated that coming to the retreat under this circumstance had helped them face many of their other fears. They talked also of their great concern for the women and children of the Muslim world, and during each gathering we sent unconditional love to them, as well as all those in fear and panic outside of our little retreat in the woods. I was certain that we were not the only group of women around the world called to send out the energy of peace and compassion to the planet at this fateful time.

Five days after the planes crashed into the World Trade Center and American life as we'd known it had changed, forty women hugged each other and went back to their families and communities.

I heard from them—one by one—how, upon returning home, they found their families and communities in what could only be described as post traumatic stress. Their own peace and rationality, not having been subjected to hourly news from the media, was able to bring their friends and family back to a place of normalcy. Each one was grateful for this opportunity she'd been given and thankful that Spirit had chosen her for this mission. I know that Mother Earth was indeed thankful that they had heeded her call.

September 21, 2001

Now, looking back at that time, there could have been so much more fear. Instead, there was a coming together of people, a unifying resolve to rise above this tragic and historic event. I have vowed to continue my work to help awaken others to the importance of the Earth. Perhaps if she had not transmuted the fear and anger, something much more tragic would have taken place. Perhaps many, many more people would have died in acts of retaliation. Perhaps this would have been the end of our lives here on Earth. We will never know. I do know that it was Mother Earth coming to our aid that held the world together this time.

I believe if we stay grounded and centered and listen to Spirit through our hearts, we will be guided through even the most terrible situations.

Thank You, Mother, for Always Being There

Chaos all around me.
Tired and weary, I run to you and curl up.
The reassuring comfort of your familiar scent fills my nostrils
as I bury my face in your breast.
You hold me while I cry, while I spit angry words,
while I finally release the pent up frustration
of being a child of yours in this fast-paced confusing world.

My brothers and sisters, as always, come to see what is wrong.
A little wren sits above me calling "Are you alright? Are you alright?"
Then the squirrels come and scold me for wallowing in self pity
on such a beautiful day.
They chase each other up and down the tree above tossing acorns at me
until I laugh and once again agree to join the human race.

"Don't stay away so long," I hear you call,
as I start off once again down the path.
I won't Mother. I'll be back soon.

Reflecting on Rain

Life isn't about how to survive the storm, but how to dance in the rain.
anonymous

Snuggled between a blueberry bush and a swamp maple, I wait out the storm. Lost in meditation, I didn't pay attention to the clouds forming to the south or the excited calling of the sparrows and wrens. Like them I usually feel the storm coming, but today my mind is far away with my sister who has left New England and followed her daughter to Louisiana in anticipation of her first grandchild. It's to be a girl, and I'll fill her head with faeries and magic, much to everyone's dismay. Baton Rouge seems so far away.

The first rain drops roused me from my reverie, and gathering up notebook and pen, I headed for the woods.

Here I sit on dry leaves from last fall. It's early summer and the oak and blueberry are green and full enough to keep out most of the rain. I watch as raindrops start to hang like little prisms on the blueberry branches. Have you ever noticed that raindrops reflect the world upside down and it is still beautiful?

Perhaps when our world seems to be turned upside down and we're complaining and fighting it, we should stop and breathe and look for the beauty that is still there.

Perhaps my sister will be fine. I know she'll be happy with her family and new granddaughter. I'll be fine too, but I'll still miss her.

Have you noticed how even the tiniest raindrop on a body of water sends endless ripples until it is stopped by the shore? Be careful what you send out from your life for it reverberates throughout the universe.

Watching a lake when it starts to rain, I've also noticed that each raindrop sends out ripples that intersect each other. The more the rain increases, the more the ripples intersect until there is chaos. It is like our own energies. We send out energy or a vibration, and it is met by the energy or vibration of another, that has been met by another, and on and on and on. We have no way of knowing if a particular person we are about to interact with has been bombarded with negative or positive energies. I vow to try my best to let it flow peacefully instead of reacting so quickly.

The next time you are by a lake on a calm day, look at the reflections. Sometimes the reflection is clearer than the reality. Sometimes the face of another person will be a clearer reflection of what vibration we are giving off than our own mind allows us to see and most times, when our world turns upside down, it can still be beautiful.

Poison Ivy

I sit among the trailing leaves of green, so tenacious that I gave up trying to clear them from my pine woods long ago. I've learned to be gentle with them and to respect them.

They are so much like the wild woman that I've become. Strong willed, tenacious, and usually considered a pest if not a downright hazard. We're both misunderstood and our virtue of protecting our environment and those around us is seldom celebrated.

Never Alone

Those who dwell among the beauties and mysteries of the Earth are never alone or weary of life.
Rachel Carson

Feeling that part of my soul is dying, I walk with leaden legs out to my beloved cornfield hoping in the solitude I can make some decisions about the rest of my life.

I've accepted the fact that my marriage has died and no amount of wishing or pleading will bring it back.

I fear leaving what I've known for 30 years, but I fear staying in a marriage that is slowly killing me and the man I still love but can no longer live with. We're on two very different paths now. We stopped communicating long ago because we simply no longer spoke the same language.

I find my way among the cinnamon ferns, now knee high. Before the summer is over they will nearly touch my shoulders. I run my fingers over their soft fuzzy green fronds enjoying their touch and think how it seems like ages since I've been touched like that by a human hand.

I follow the winding little path through the ferns dappled in sunlight, feeling some comfort from the familiar hardwood forest.

Swamp maples, oak trees, and an occasional pine or cedar fill this portion of the acreage behind my house. It was once a home.

I make it as far as the stone wall at the edge of the field and sit, head in hands, weeping and trying to figure out what to do next. I'm so deep inside myself I don't notice the red dragonfly that flies over to my hand. From the corner of my eye I notice what looks like a red jewel on my finger. Blinking back the tears I encounter two green eyes staring up at me. He flies up and touches my lip and then lands back on my hand. Peering at me, I finally pour my heart out to this little creature. He continues to sit patiently until I stop crying and come to some kind of inner resolve. Satisfied that I'm alright, he flies off across the field.

Was he sent by God? Was he God? He was a reminder that I am never truly alone and help will always be there when I ask for it. I gather myself up, and decision made, step fearlessly back on the path and into a day that will change my life forever.

A Walking Meditation

[Nature] is the one place miracles not only happen,
but happen all the time.
Thomas Wolfe, American novelist

Spring, O Glorious Spring: a time that signifies rebirth, a chance to begin again. What better time to start working on my body, mind, and spirit.

I think, as I stride past red and yellow tulips bursting forth, how I want to share this bright beautiful morning with everyone. My spirit is lifted as I breathe in peace and beauty and breathe out the deep rumblings of fear and anxiety. It was a perfect day to once again start my daily walking meditations. Being a healer, I have chosen to stay in a place of peace and love through these trying times in order to help those who come through my door or cross my path find relief from the anxiety and stress that is so prevalent.

Walking meditations are perfect for those of us who find it hard to sit still for any length of time. I find them more effective than sitting quietly focused inward. Moving along, step by step, out in the world, I feel a deep sense of connection to all living things. It is the continuous rhythm of my feet that allows my mind to clear so that I may hear my soul's messages. Some of the most confusing problems have been solved while striding along in the fresh air.

This form of meditation has been used since the beginnings of recorded history. Ancient monasteries often had labyrinths where monks were expected to pace and meditate in order to achieve a sense of connection to God. I recently read that people who incorporate at least 15 minutes of walking meditation into their life daily, report a new, more positive outlook. I can certainly attest to that. It makes me feel wonderful and optimistic. The more positive we feel, the healthier we are. Walking, breathing, and being in sunlight helps to boost my immune system while I relieve stress.

The only preparation I need is to get out of bed and put on comfortable shoes. I take a moment to stand silently, feel the sun and air on my skin, listen to and smell the world around me. I give thanks for the beautiful day and all my blessings and start off. This is not a race. I take a moment to find my own natural gait and focus on my feet connecting to the Earth or my breath going in and out. As thoughts cross my mind, I just let them go and tell myself I'll think about them later, if it's necessary. Sometimes I use the time to put specific thoughts or affirmations into my mind by repeating over and over a positive message such as "I'm healthy and happy" or "the world is an abundant place, I have all that I need." Today, I'm just striding along feeling the air on my skin and sun warming my face. I feel wonderful.

I've found that a short meditative walk each day, whether in the morning or in the evening after a long day, offers an easy, cost-free way to maintain health and fitness in my body, in my mind and most importantly, in my spirit.

Oh, Great Spirit, thank you for this beautiful day. Thank you for my beautiful body and thank you for my clear mind. Let me use this energy wisely and as a gift to help others.

The Great Plant Hunt

If the day and the night are such that you greet them with joy, and life emits a fragrance like flowers and sweet scented herbs, is more elastic, more starry, more immortal—that is your success.
Henry David Thoreau

Memorial Day has passed and once again it's time for "The Annual Plant Hunt." I arrive at my friend Val's house early with coffee in hand and my van empty, ready to be filled with the treasures of the day. It's not uncommon for us to arrive back home after dusk, having covered a 50-mile radius searching for the perfect plants for our gardens.

This year I've given some careful thought to what I might be searching for. Blessed for years with acres of land to play with, I chose plants with gay abandon: all sizes, colors, smells and forms. Having moved to a city apartment this winter, with a front yard the size of my front hallway, I have to be a little less reckless. I will still return with many more than I need, but the ones that call to me the loudest will find their way into my van and those that cannot fit in my tiny garden will be given away.

This year I have a plan, very uncommon for this wild woman but a necessity, and I believe it will work. I've decided to choose plants that serve a number of purposes. I've always planted many herbs as well as flowers and vegetables. What I need to look for are herbs that have medicinal qualities as well as wonderful flavor for cooking—colorful flowers would be nice, too.

After much contemplation, trying not to sacrifice flavor for health benefits or color, I've come up with a small number of plants that will make a very beautiful garden, bloom all summer, and require very little maintenance.

First on my list is basil. It's been recommended for just about every conceivable ailment and it tastes wonderful, smells wonderful, and comes in a variety of colors. I'll plant it at the base of a colorful cherry tomato and enjoy it in my salads and in pesto.

Garlic is one of the most powerful healing herbs, being a super antibiotic. It's a wonderful herb for cooking and has a pretty flower so that will fit into my garden too.

Parsley is pretty and will look nice planted with flowers. I can make it into tea, munch on it to freshen my breath, and sprinkle it on food to add a little color and big nutrition.

I love fragrant rosemary and its pale blue flowers. Maybe I'll get the creeping variety this year to hang over the sides of my pots. I love it with chicken or hamburgers on the grill. It actually acts as a food preservative, so it is great to put in mayonnaise-based salads for picnics.

I have to have thyme. Maybe I'll plant some of the moss-like variety in the cracks of the sidewalk in front of the old brownstone where I live, so each passerby will get a little gift of scent. I know I'd be delighted. A little lemon thyme tucked into one of the pots will give me plenty to go with chicken or fish.

I can't forget sage, another natural antibiotic. It comes in a variety of colors and scents and I dry the leaves for my bread stuffing. Fresh sage in omelets chopped up with all the other herbs. Yummm. I think I'll get a few different kinds. I love the dusty gray, but the green and white variety is nice, and then there is lemon sage . . . and didn't I see a deep purple last year, too?

I have plant fever for sure and had better end my list. Many more interesting little plants will call to me and find their way into the van and I'll have to send them to foster homes, but only to the best where they'll be well tended with love.

I sit here and picture my garden planted in many shades of green with pots of yellow and gold nasturtiums to compliment the red of my cherry tomatoes. Their bright blossoms will add a peppery, colorful "bite" to my salads.

Oh, what a glorious adventure I'm about to embark upon! I know that each morning when I walk out my door, I'll be greeted with a feast for the senses and food for my soul. I can't think of a better way to start my days.

Peru – The Heart of Mother Earth

For years, I'd felt a deep longing to go to Peru. Even in my nightly dreams, flying on the back of a golden eagle, I'd soar over the green continent of South America and, to my dismay, end up on a dry, arid island somewhere in the middle of the ocean.

I was taken by surprise the day the phone rang in my office and an unfamiliar voice asked, "Is this Linda Hogan?"

"Yes . . ." I replied, feeling a strange sensation as if the world had just stopped.

Her next words were: "We'd like to send you to Peru for two weeks, all expenses paid, to see if you would be interested in leading other women there on travel adventures."

"Yes, yes, yes!" I exclaimed. "Without a doubt!"

"Good," she laughed. "I'll put the ticket in the mail to you today with the itinerary. You'll leave in three weeks, fly into Lima, and meet a group of healers from California and our guide, Jorge. He'll take care of everything from there."

It seemed the most natural thing in the world to me: get on an airplane (which I had never done before), fly alone to a foreign country (knowing only a few words that would get me fed and to a restroom), and then find my way in the middle of the night to a hotel in Lima to find a group of people I'd never met. Strangely, I felt no anxiety—only excitement.

A week later, Andrea, the owner of the travel company, called to see how I was doing.

"Andrea, I have the strangest sensation that someone, or something, knows I'm coming," I replied.

"Yes, of course," she answered. "It's the Apus, they're the ones that have been calling you."

"Apus?" I asked. "Is that an Indian tribe?"

Andrea laughed and said not to worry; I'd meet them in Peru.

Flying over South America at dawn, the gentleman in the seat next to me grabbed my shoulder, pointed out the window at mountains shining in the distance, and said "Look, Leeenda, the Apus."

"*Si*, Jose," I answered, "They have been calling me."

"*Muy bueno*," he replied, and went back to sleep.

This first trip to Peru was an incredible experience: walking beside and learning from shaman Jorge Luis Delgado, participating in a ceremony by Q'ero medicine men, trekking in Machu Picchu with only the full moon and Jorge to guide us, connecting to Pachamama and the sacred Apus, and meeting other healers from California who shared healing techniques not yet heard of on the East Coast. It was a dream I had never dared to dream that had come true.

I vowed to return . . . and I did two years later.

The second time, I traveled with my friend, June, and Jose Luis Herrera, a Peruvian shaman and founder of Rainbow Jaguar Expeditions. More wonderful experiences in the Sacred Valley with the Q'ero medicine people and more intense ceremonies drawing me closer and closer to Mother Earth (or *Pachamama* as she is called in Peru) would forever alter my life as I had known it.

I've learned of the infinite wisdom and power of the Earth and of the beautiful people, the indigenous who hold her sacred. I do my best to live each day as a shaman by respecting the Earth and all of her creatures and doing whatever I can to help all.

When you give your life over to Spirit as I did so many years ago, and you stop trying to control everything, just letting your life flow gently, each day becomes a beautiful adventure. You have no idea where you're going, but you know it will be wonderful when you get there. You also have no doubt that it is exactly where you're meant to be and that Mother Earth will take care of you just as she promised.

Sacred Silence

Urubamba, Peru
July 1, 2004

I sit in silence.

I sit in silence like I've never known.

I sit in silence like I've never known peace.

I sit in silence like I've never known peace in my soul.

I sit in Silence.

A silence where you can hear butterfly wings.

A silence where you can hear butterfly wings and a leaf fall from a tree.

A silence and peace I have looked for forever.

I hear only Pachamama.

A breeze rustles the dried leaves of a tree where a tiny sparrow quietly chirps as if afraid to break the sacred silence of this old monastery. A small fat bird, brown with a white band at his throat, sits and converses with me. The white band gives him a toothy grin. His song is not melodious; he sits there and calls only, "Be! Be!" Open your eyes and *be* in the moment. The small bird reminds me to see what I have and to be grateful.

A hummingbird feeds on the pink geranium in front of me reminding me to take time to sip the nectar and sweetness from life.

The Apus change before my eyes. I sit dwarfed below these magical mountains of the Andes, so alive they have personalities. They appear to move in the distance as Inti shines down upon their peaks bathing them in golden light.

Everyone is still napping and I am in this holy sanctuary alone. Shangri-la. Yes! In this silence, I contemplate how each of us, in this holy life, is truly alone. Can we be aware of the Shangri-la in which we live without first going outside the gates to witness the strife and struggle?

Perhaps it is in moments of strife that our eyes and hearts are truly opened so we can recognize times of true beauty and peace and know our own sacred Shangri-la is always there . . . just beyond the veil . . . when we make time, release our fears and step through.

The Way of the Shaman Is Balance

If we are peaceful, if we are happy, we can smile and blossom like a flower, and everyone in our family, our entire society, will benefit from our peace.
Thich Nhat Hanh

My love of the Earth has led me to study with shamans and medicine people from many cultures.

Walking along well-worn roads made of dirt or stone, where my feet connect to the Earth, fills me with a sense of joy and peace. It is a feeling of being home. Home and deeply connected to this planet that I love.

The indigenous cultures that I've visited still live off the land and rely upon her for sustenance. These are people who build their own homes from the clay and mud they have dug from the land. They mix it with hay from the fields and water from the rivers and form it into bricks with their hands. They plant gardens with seeds that they've saved or traded. They plow with sticks or animals. They treasure the water from the rivers that run through their villages, for it quenches their thirst and waters their animals. They mix it with the rich Earth to form bricks for their homes, and they wash their clothes in it. The Earth is their life support; they are thankful and grateful. These are people who seem to have nothing, but they smile and laugh as they go about their work and are happy to share whatever they have with you even if you are a stranger. We could learn so much from them.

Living off the land and depending on nature creates respect for living creatures, even though they sometimes have to be killed for survival. Waste is taboo and not tolerated. It is an insult to Father Sky and Mother Earth, the two core beings in shamanic cultures. The people are very careful to show respect to the Earth and elements, knowing they cannot survive without good weather and hunting.

The relationship with nature is seen as one of interdependence, rather than exploitation. This reverence for the natural world has allowed for survival of indigenous cultures on their lands for thousands of years without degradation of their environment. As western civilization forces its ways upon these cultures, the threat of losing this connection to the Earth and the joy these people have known is being replaced with frustration and discontent. Crimes are on the rise and there has been fighting and alienation among these once peaceful peoples.

Juan, a sweet friend of mine, a Q'ero medicine person from Peru, told me with a broken heart of how he and the other healers of his village were being driven out. Missionaries had hiked the three days up the mountain to his village, built a church and school, and then threatened to take down the school unless all the villagers promised to give up their ancient religion and ways. The shamans—healers and holy men and women—were told they were no longer needed and driven out of town.

If we can learn to live in *balance* with the Earth and each other once again—interdependently, instead of through exploitation—I believe we can perhaps experience what Heaven on Earth is all about.

In indigenous cultures, the shaman's duty is that of social worker, as well as healer. He or she keeps his or her eyes open for trouble and sees where there is a need. Shamans can be found helping to build a house, encouraging others to send food to a sick neighbor or babysitting, as well as performing physical and spiritual healings.

If we could all see the Earth and her people through the eyes of a shaman, we too would embrace Gaia, Mother Earth, Pachamama . . . the beautiful planet we live on. If we could learn from her, we would provide for and offer protection to her, as well as her people.

I've challenged myself to look from the heart and eyes of a shaman to see what really needs to be done in my community and do it. I've learned that when I help others, I am always paid back with so much love from the Earth and universe that it overwhelms me.

The Shaman in Your Cupboard

I never realized the effect of melodies until I began to change what I listened to. A simple melody that has helped me many days, is the melody of nature. When I am able to hear it outside from my swing, I often find myself becoming lost in the bird songs.
Rev. Ashira Goddard

I will be forever thankful to my indigenous teachers and the knowledge they've shared with me . . .

The Earth provides us with a beautiful, healing energy of which most are unaware. Connecting to the Earth's energy is as simple as sitting outside and relaxing. I've noticed that people who spend a lot of time outdoors look and feel healthier. One of the great benefits is that any depression or anger soon leaves. Nature is the natural antidepressant. I now walk with a lighter step and have less joint pain thanks to Mother Earth. That's why magnetic therapy is so popular these days. People spend less time outside in the Earth's magnetic field so they need to pay practitioners or buy products to replenish their supply. This is a great alternative, but I prefer being outdoors.

Studying and working with a Native American medicine woman, as well as shamans from Peru and Brazil, I have learned many simple but powerful techniques using the gifts of the Earth that anyone can use to improve their health and well-being. These practices have been used for thousands of years by indigenous healers worldwide and are of great benefit to anyone looking to return to a more natural way of life. With the use of minerals, plants and essential oils, you can fight almost any virus or bacteria.

When plagued with a headache, or ache or pain, I listen to the voice of the natural world.

It not only distracts me, but raises my vibration and attunes me to the energy of Mother Earth.

Simply relaxing by a stream, forest, field or any natural setting, and focusing on the sounds of nature refreshes and heals.

⚜

Have you ever noticed that you feel drained or full of tension after being around negative people? When I can't avoid them, I know how to help prevent the effects of their drain on my energy. We all pick up the energy of others whether it's positive and uplifting or negative and draining.

Salt and stones, two of my favorite healing tools, absorb negative energy. I keep a bowl of sea salt on my desk, or in any room where tension sometimes builds. I have a basket of small beach pebbles that I've collected on my desk, which I periodically run my fingers through.

Salt and stones also absorb pain. Grandmother Maryanne, an Algonquin medicine woman, taught me to make a bag of white cotton cloth and fill it with salt. I use this bag on toothaches, muscle aches or for headaches. Smooth stones rubbed on a sprain will soon relieve it. Using arnica oil with the stones works even better.

When I'm feeling particularly agitated or anxious, I take a handful of sea salt into the shower with me and gently massage it all over my body. It absorbs the tension and negative energy I've picked up and washes it down the drain. I'm left with a healthy glow too. Soaking in an epsom salts bath is another great way to relieve muscular tension and get toxins out of your body. Keep the water running; it changes the ions and also helps in the detoxification process. I keep a small mesh bag of small stones that I've collected and take in the tub with me to pull out the negative energy.

I love stones. I have been working with them my entire life and have developed a working relationship with them. Remember the pet rocks of the '60s? I have herds of stones. They're in my pockets, in my car, in my handbags. They travel with me and if someone is moving and can't take their favorite stones, I adopt them. Stones are *good*. If one calls to you . . . pick it up! It has a special healing property that you need or a subconscious message for you.

Gaia is a nurturing mother who wants her children to be healthy and thrive. She willingly provides us with everything we need to sustain ourselves physically, emotionally, and spiritually.

The Frog Whisperer

Worlds can be found by a child and an adult bending down and looking together under the grass stems or at the skittering crabs in a tidal pool.
Mary Catherine Bateson, American anthropologist

Oh, what a gift God has given me! Ever since I was a little girl, I've felt more at home outdoors than in any house. The woods and fields have been my home since I could remember with wild creatures my family and friends.

I grew up in a wonderful family and my mother encouraged each of us to be who we truly are. My younger sister wore fluffy dresses and the more petticoats she could fit under her full skirts the happier she was. She was quiet and neat and a little lady. My older brother was a dancer and danced on Broadway at one point in his life.

And then there was me, my mother's wild child. She dressed me in red every day because she said it was easier to spot me in the tree tops. From the tops of trees, I could see the world and I dreamed of one day traveling farther than my eyes could see. I spent hours every day outside playing with bugs and any creature that would tolerate me.

I devised a plan one day to train mice. These were not your caged, white mice from any pet shop; these were the field mice that frequented our chicken coop. I would see them eating the cracked corn for the chickens and rooster, but they'd scurry away when I came in. I reasoned that if I was the one providing the cracked corn they'd come to me. I'd see them hiding behind buckets or peeking out at me from holes in the wall, but they wouldn't come close.

One day, I went to the chicken coop, covered myself in corn, then waited . . . and waited. I'd see them looking, but they just wouldn't come close. Being a determined little girl, who did not give up easily, I went day after day and sat quietly, without moving. Each day, they came a little closer until one day, the first mouse came into my lap, took some food, and scurried away to his nest. The next day, there was another mouse. Soon, I had families of mice waiting for me. I was thrilled, to say the least.

I dreamed of joining a circus one day and taming lions. At the supper table, I'd tell my family of my adventures taming wild animals and they laughed. My father would question my mother about my wild imagination and imply it might get me into trouble some day.

One day, lost in conversing with mice, I didn't hear my mother calling me. She opened the door to the chicken coop and found me sitting on the floor among chickens and little mice. Rodents, she called them.

"What are you doing with those rodents?" She didn't sound angry; she just shook her head and told me to go take a bath. She told my father and I was given a lecture about germs and polio and forbidden to go there again. A boy in our neighborhood had polio and now had to be pushed in a wheelchair. Thoughts of losing my independence was enough to keep me from the chicken coop; but to this day, I love little mice and when my own daughter asked for one, we picked him out together.

It was one humid day decades later, sitting by a brook, that I first recognized my gift as a "frog whisperer." As a child, I'd try to catch frogs for hours. Sometimes their slimly little bodies would be held for a moment before slipping from my fingers.

My last escapade with frogs had been the last day of my senior year in high school, when one of the football players in my class asked if I wanted to cut English class and go catch bullfrogs with him. I was thrilled because he was pretty cute, and he later was thrilled because I seemed to have a talent for catching frogs. In a matter of ten minutes, we'd caught six really big bullfrogs. Throwing them in a book bag, we headed back for class.

Always looking very sweet and angelic, I walked into my Algebra class, sat down, and opened the book bag. Soon the frogs were hopping down the aisles, students were laughing—or screaming. Mrs. Coyle was red in the face and (pardon the pun) hopping mad.

Frogs had not been part of my life for a very long time now, but on this warm, humid day, as I sat gazing into the brook, I saw two glassy little orbs looking back at me. I looked deeper into the water and saw that this frog was like none I had ever seen before. It was a warm, cream color with iridescent gold markings drawn around each eye and down his back. I stared at him and he stared at me.

Thinking to myself, I said, *Why don't you just hop right over here and visit with me?* To my astonishment, he swam to the edge of the brook and hopped up on the embankment!

Come here and let me have a look at you, I thought as I put my hand down. With two hops he was at my hand and I gently scooped him up and raised him to eye level. Strange as it may seem, we gazed lovingly at each other for quite some time. He truly was beautiful with his markings of liquid gold. I have no idea what he thought of me.

Yes, the fantasy of a frog prince did cross my mind and I'll admit to giving him a little kiss. Much to my dismay I didn't turn into a frog, nor he a prince. He just sat there contentedly on the palm of my hand.

I finally put him down at the edge of the brook expecting him to dive back into the water, but he turned around and came up the bank to me again. I didn't pick him up this time, but just sat there meditating with him beside me. Fifteen minutes later, I opened my eyes to find him gone. I looked for him up and down the brook but never saw him again.

Another afternoon on a visit to a local garden center with my friend Cat (short for Catherine), we came upon a large fountain shaded by a huge rhododendron bush. Over on the far side were some frogs.

"Would you like to see something magic?" I secretively asked her. Once again, I spoke to the little creatures with my mind. *Will you come over here and see us?* I thought. Over they swam to our side of the fountain. *Would you like us to scratch your heads?* I asked them silently. The two little frogs stretched their front legs, lifting their heads out of the water and we scratched the tops of their heads.

"You're a frog whisperer, my friend," Cat said.

Ah, yes, I thought, *there is a huge calling for frog whisperers.*

I've found that when I'm deeply connected to the Earth, all of her creatures feel that I am one with them or part of the universe. Do I really appear as one of them or as some natural part of the surroundings? Do I become the log or rock I'm sitting on? I can't answer these questions; but in any case, I know I am perceived as non-threatening and inviting. This was the beginning of my animal adventures.

Perhaps this gift does not seem particularly useful to most. I am only now beginning to use this talent in a way others may value. My wellness center is in a lovely location on a lake. I share the building with two other businesses. In the summer, it is most pleasant to walk to the side of the lake for a break and change of scenery.

I've been in this location for three years now. The first two years I was excited to witness the courtship of the local geese, followed by the parading about of fuzzy little goslings. The only problem was that as these babies grew up, our yard became the headquarters for a flock of 33 geese. Geese are fun to watch, but they are messy and what goes in comes out immediately. I would hose off the patio every morning, but it became impossible for any of us to venture to the edge of the water. The yard became off limits during spring and summer.

We tried chasing them away and making loud noises, but to no avail. As soon as we left for the day, the yard became the picnic grounds for gaggles of geese. This year, when the first two geese flew in, I went and sat by the edge of the shore and had a talk with them. I explained to them that we too needed to use the yard, that we'd been patient for two years, and now it was our turn. They were not to come in and use the yard—and if they did, they would have to suffer the consequences. I suggested strongly that they find another place to mate and gather.

I thought nothing more of it until my landlord asked "What did you do with the geese?" I laughed and said I had a talk with them. Whether it had anything to do with our conversation or not—but I believe it did—they have moved to the other side of the lake. We've seen them swimming around out there, diving for fish and sunning themselves, but they have not come ashore. We can walk freely in the yard now without having to come in and change shoes. Perhaps next year, I will market myself as a goose whisperer.

We Are All One

When we try to pick out anything by itself, we find it hitched to everything else in the Universe.
John Muir, American environmentalist

Often, my encounters with nature teach me a lesson I need to learn. Walking in an early spring cornfield one day, I notice what seems to be a moving clump of mud. It blends perfectly with the freshly plowed field and I have to rub my eyes to make sure that what I am seeing is really moving. As it gets closer I see that it is a large turtle with mud caked to her shell. I move down to eye level and she looks at me as I peer at her. Having recently had the "frog experiences," I want so badly to touch her.

Please let me touch you, I ask silently. I reach over and touched the top of her head. She blinks her eyes and starts moving again. I reach over to touch her again and in an instant she grabs me with her powerful jaws and just as quickly lets me go. Her bite is hard enough to give me a slight cut and make an impression, but not hard enough to really hurt me. In that instant, I clearly hear her say, "Respect boundaries. Do not interfere with the missions of others."

Chastised, I watch as she waddles away to lay her eggs somewhere in the newly plowed Earth.

Today, it is incredibly beautiful in the cornfield behind my house. I have been watching the sky lately. It is definitely different, almost transparent and ethereal, with clouds of different and unusual shapes. Spirit has been speaking loudly to me through Mother Earth and her creatures.

My first message came from butterflies, a tiny blue azure and a black swallowtail, flying, landing and posing in front of me. "Your true beauty cannot be shown until you spread your wings."

The second message came as I sat on my meditation stone trying to "just be." It was from a swarm of mosquitoes and a fly. "Your unrelenting determination sometimes causes others to view you as a pest."

As I walked in the newly plowed Earth, I was reminded, "Through the eyes of love, we can see beauty in all things."

The fourth message was from a red-tailed hawk circling overhead. "Fly into the current, ride the spiral up, and soar effortlessly."

Stopping to pick stinging nettles on my way back to the house, I was reminded to stay grounded and connected to the Earth. "Be deliberate and grasp you dreams firmly or they may reach out and bite you."

I've had squirrels sit beside me eating acorns while I sat and meditated on a log. Another time, while sitting at the edge of the lake outside my office, a muskrat swam up and started pulling grass from around my feet. I'm always taken aback by the familiarity of these creatures who seem not to care the least that I am there . . . and my heart sings because of it.

The indigenous elders I have spent time with always stress that civilization's problems would soon be solved if we relearned to respect and see spirit in all things. I have been told that those of us who have made a conscious connection to the Earth will find it easier to survive the predicted Earth changes. Those of us who "hear" and "see" nature will receive the knowledge that we need to take care of ourselves and others.

꧁ ꧂

Strolling the grounds of the old monastery the other day with my friend Roland, we laughed as bright green grasshoppers jumped along beside us. I'm sure I heard them say, "The road is open before you. Jump fearlessly into the unknown, you are not alone. Many like you are taking great leaps of faith. There is no time to waste."

We know we are blessed. We've taken leaps of faith in allowing others to be witness to our communication with other worlds: Roland, with his head in the heavens speaking with angels and those who have passed; and me, with my feet deep in the Earth surrounded by nature spirits and communing with all of her creatures.

Perhaps others hearing our stories will allow their own hearts to open, so they too can experience those same feelings of great love and support the universe so generously offers.

The Monastery

Moving to the city, after seventeen years of walking out my door to nature and one hundred acres of undeveloped land, has taken a toll on me. I knew I'd miss it, but maybe not this much. After all, I do have a lake and small yard at my healing center, and I'm happy living in the city with a beautiful park across the street. It's adequate, but I just can't lose myself in it for hours like I used to.

When my new friend Jerrilyn invited me to go walking in the woods with her, her husband Dan, and their two dogs, I accepted gratefully. It was a beautiful day and I longed to be outdoors. I'd finished my work and when they arrived, I jumped in the backseat of their car with a big greyhound and a tiny whippet. After being licked all over by both of them, we set off.

Twenty minutes later, we arrived at the Cumberland Monastery, the former home to Cistercian monks, a silent order commonly known as the Trappists. Fire had destroyed most of the beautiful old granite building. The monks had relocated and turned the property over to the city of Cumberland, which built a library and now maintain the fields and trails for public use.

Dogs pulling on leashes, we set off down the trail that led through a pine forest and into a field. I felt myself relax and enjoyed the brisk walk. I took it all in that day. Beautiful forests and swamps and ponds, trails up and down hills, and little paths invited me deeper into the woods. I felt at home once again and remembered the message given to me from my favorite tree before I said good-bye for what would be the last time: *Remember, when you sit under any tree in silence and meditation, you will be sitting under me.* I knew I'd be returning soon to explore and make the acquaintance of the nature spirits and animals.

It was a wonderful day with my friends, and I'll thank them forever for introducing me to this special place where I will be able to reconnect to Mother Earth once again.

Walking on a Fall Day

In every walk with Nature, one receives far more than he seeks.
John Muir, American environmentalist

Windblown hair, lips stained purple from wild grapes, I smile at this beautiful woman in the mirror.

Free enough to leave my work behind and heed the call of Grandfather Wind, I had driven the twenty minutes to the Monastery, wind pushing my car and adding to the excitement that was building.

You *are* a crazy wild woman, you know—but it's been entirely too long since you've played in the wind.

Few people are at the Monastery, and I seem to be the only one heading to the trails in the woods.

"Be careful, young lady," a gentleman older than myself says. "The woods are dangerous today." I think to myself how not being in the woods is dangerous most days, and smile because he calls me young lady . . . instead of ma'am.

I enter the woods, gigantic oaks swaying in the strong wind. I have a moment of apprehension as I remember the old man's words and entertain the possibility of a dead branch landing on my head.

I find a cozy, less-threatening spot under some low branched beeches and sit for a moment to connect to the Earth and breathe in the wonderful energy of the approaching storm. I am connected and I am safe, and the fear leaves me.

I hear the chatter of small birds, but the only ones brave or crazy enough to be flying today are the crows. Magic birds . . . like me. I walk along on the deserted trails, feeling as if I own the woods. Groupings of boulders, or groves of pine trees, draw me off the main trail onto little paths. Here is where I look for the magic.

I spy a tree, still alive, but with a hollow trunk. When you look closely, it is a perfect little fairy house. I look for fairies, but find instead a green bug beautiful enough to be a fairy wearing an emerald green iridescent shell. Perhaps it is a fairy in disguise. I watch him and send him lots of love, and he sends his appreciation back to me.

I follow the small path back to the main trail and listen to the wind. I can almost hear voices. I listen hard, maybe too hard, and can almost make out what they are saying.

This is a sign that I've been away from the forest too long. I no longer hear the whisperings of Mother Nature as easily as I used to. I vow to stay in touch and meander on my way again.

My foot slips on something round and hard. I look down to find hickory nuts littering the path. What a find. I crack the leathery green shell and out pops a hard little tan nut. I know that it will take pounding with a really large rock to crack these shells, but I put a handful in my pocket anyway. I slip an equal amount from their green coats to leave for the squirrels and go along my way.

The trail leads out of the woods and into a field of goldenrods and little wild asters. Here the wind pushes me along and plays with my hair. I see the clouds getting darker and starting to fill the sky and wonder if I'll make it back before the storm. The wind makes me want to fly. Maybe flying would be dangerous; even the hawks I usually see soaring above me in these fields are grounded today.

Something white and sparkling amongst the brown of the field catches my eye. I believe they are feathers, but when I get closer discover that they are the opened seed pods of milkweed.

I pick up a handful, blow wishes for health, happiness, and prosperity into them for everyone in the world and toss it into the wind. I watch it separate into hundreds of little iridescent blessings and know that this is what fairies look like when dancing.

I inhale as deeply as I can, bringing the energy of the wind and impending storm into my body to revitalize it. Asking that Grandfather Wind blow away any tension and emotions that I need to release, I inhale again and the fragrance of wild grapes fills my soul.

I spy the grape vines behind a protective barrier of briars. Not to be daunted, I maneuver around the wild roses and stand on tiptoes to reach the purple grapes. A briar pricks me briefly and says, "Don't be greedy," and then lets me go. I take only a handful and pop one into my mouth. The warm little purple globe pops in my mouth and I delight in its sweet, silky flesh. I chew the skin until it is too sour and spit it out with the seeds. Ah, look at all that Mother Earth has provided for me. I could feast all day on nuts and grapes and other wild berries and make a salad from the wild greens I've seen.

I feel safe, happy, and content now. I find my way back to the parking area and my car and discover a gift has been left for me. There by the door is a crow feather. A reminder that there is magic everywhere . . . you need only take the time to look.

Thank you, Mother, for always being there.

Sepia Woods of November

*Authentic spirituality awakens the soul, reconnects us with the sacred,
and fills us with the passion of life. Spiritual development is not about
religious rituals and practices, it is about waking up to the wonder of life.*
David N. Elkins

Walking the monastery trails silently, hands folded beneath my green wool cape, as holy men had years before, I walk with them in silent meditation and devotion, sure that in some past lifetime I, too, have taken their vows of silence and poverty and service to the land.

Have you ever sat in a sepia forest? Everywhere I gaze, shades of brown and gray with an occasional birch standing out against the monotone day gives the feeling of being in an old photograph.

I love November woods. Trees with most of their leaves fallen, showing their true personalities, celebrate that I am here and remind me to be my authentic self and not the person I suppose others would wish me to be.

Although the main trails at the Monastery are empty of people and I'm assured of a most peaceful walk, something about the woods beckons me today and I choose a side trail littered with leaves that crunch beneath my boots. I question if there is ever really a wrong path, and wonder if we eventually end up at the same place in the end, with different lessons learned from our detours.

I'm fearless in the woods, especially today with "Monks of Old" as my companions, and take one winding path after another. I have never been so deep into the grounds and am surprised when I come upon heaps of roughly carved granite blocks. I can almost see the silent, heavily robed monks working diligently to form blocks for the monastery walls, each swing of the hammer an act of love as the big, sturdy draft horses hitched to the wagon wait patiently.

I wander further down the path and soon feel drawn to climb over the stone wall and into the woods. Ahead, deeper in the woods, I see a large shape I can't quite make out and go to explore. It is a very huge boulder, dropped by a glacier eons ago. I climb to the top and sit looking through the gray woods into the green field where I normally walk.

From my perch, I can see that I am the only one walking the trails this fine day. I sit alone in the woods, high on a rock and feel as if I'm Queen of the Forest. The surrounding trees lean toward me, excited and happy that I am here. They applaud and shake their branches and birds twitter. I bow deeply and thank them.

From my perch I notice a yellow glow, uncommon in these gray woods, that entices me to go further. Climbing precariously from my throne, I wander toward the glow and discover a grove of beech trees, their sunny yellow leaves just starting to fall, lighting up this chill November morning. Their color gives warmth and I lay down at their feet, connecting to Mother Earth, clearing myself of negative energy and allowing her warm healing energy to renew my tired spirit.

As yellow leaves blanket me, I silently ask the question in my heart one more time. "Who am I?" Surprised, this time I hear an answer. It is strong and clear: *You are a Witness and Keeper of the Land.* You witness God's creations, acknowledge them with reverence, and in so doing you heal the planet and everything on it. Do not take this position lightly. Few are chosen and it is a position of great responsibility. Like the monks who once tilled this land and tended this forest, your only reward and acknowledgment will be the love you feel in your own heart from being a humble servant to Spirit.

And that will be enough.

Sharing the Winter Wonder

One kind word can warm three winter months.
Japanese proverb

Hiking boots laced, layers of warm clothes under my windbreaker, I leave the warmth of my city apartment and head for the woods. Few people have ventured out on this snowy Sunday morning as I crawl and skid down side roads to the main street and find my way to the highway. My usual twenty minute ride will take at least thirty this morning, but it's well worth it for the intense pleasure of being the first to make tracks on the pristine snow of the Monastery trails.

The gates are open and I drive in and park. I find two cars there with drivers sipping hot coffees that steam up their windows. Dogs run around chasing each other nearby.

I get to the trail head anticipating that first step into the silent woods blanked in new white snow.

My breath is taken away, not by the splendor of it all, but by the realization that many before me have come to walk the white trails. My trails! I'm indignant for a moment as I stand there staring at the well trod path. Little people feet, big people feet, dog feet. Where have they all come from? I've walked these woods, spring, summer and fall, and rarely seen another. I've often lamented how sad it is that I am the only one who enjoys these woodland trails.

I start up the trail, wondering about these mysterious fellow nature lovers that I seldom see. They're not here now. Perhaps they live nearby and came before breakfast and are now curled up with the Sunday paper in a cozy kitchen. Perhaps there are still a few in the woods ahead of me. My consternation at not being the first to hike in these snowy woods today leaves and is replaced by a warm feeling in my heart, a good feeling. I'm not alone. There really are others out there, lovers of the outdoors just like me but on different schedules. Tree huggers and dog walkers and maybe even a frog whisperer or two. Life is good.

Once again I am humbled and reminded that I am not one of a kind. I do have a tribe. I am not alone.

We are never alone and Mother Earth wants us to remember that "we are one."

Message in the Clouds

Clouds come from time to time—
and bring a chance to rest
from looking at the moon.
Basho, Japanese Haiku poet

Oh, what a glorious winter day to be here at the Monastery! I smell a hint of spring in the air this morning; although temperatures hover around 35 degrees and there is snow and ice underfoot as I head for a field, I know will be bathed in sun. There it is, but snow still blankets most of it. My vision of sprawling out on the dried grass letting the sun bathe me as I drift off to a tropical island will need to be postponed.

In one far corner, I spy a patch of brown next to a flat black rock, a perfect place to sit and contemplate my plans for this new year. I trod through the snow over to this haven warmed by the sun and spread my small woven mat upon the stone which still holds the winter cold.

I feel eager for this new year. I've consciously released the old attitudes and relationships holding me back. I'm almost ready to charge ahead fearlessly. I say "almost" because in all truth, I'm still not sure exactly what or where I'm charging to. I've been still long enough. I feel a call to travel west, but question if it is because sun and heat beating off of red rocks seem so much more inviting than Rhode Island winters. I know I will be traveling. I feel like perhaps it is a year to gain more knowledge.

I sit with eyes closed soaking up the sun—feeling, I imagine, much like the turtles I see sunning on logs in the pond every spring.

Opening my eyes, I gaze at the cornflower blue sky with clouds that send me a message to remind me that whatever lies ahead is magic. Wishing I had brought my camera, I search in my bag and find a pencil and scrap of paper. Above me, formed by clouds, is an eagle. Tucked under his outstretched wing is the head of a jaguar. Starting below them, and reaching into a huge cloud above, is the tail of a dragon. Ah, power and wisdom surrounded by protection and magic.

It is a good message and one that reminds me to believe in myself. I have all the power and wisdom I need to find my way in this world and whatever brings joy and magic into my life is the path I should follow. And I will.

Call of the Ravens

If Raven has come into your life, expect MAGIC.

Raven speaks of the opportunity to become the magician and/or enchantress of your life. Each of us has a magician within, and it is Raven which can show us how to bring that part of us out of the dark into the light. Raven speaks of messages from the spirit realm that can shapeshift your life dramatically. Raven teaches how to take that which is unformed and give it the form your desire.
Ted Andrews, *Animal-Speak*

It had been two years of endings.

It started with the dissolution of my marriage of 33 years. Then the sale of the house my children had grown up in and the need to leave my true home: the beloved woods and fields that I had cared for, protected, and turned to for solace and comfort. I moved my earthly goods from the country to the city and had just started to settle in when I received the ultimate blow: the death of my beautiful spirited 93-year-old mother, the one person who loved me unconditionally and celebrated my wildness.

It was early March when the raven first appeared.

I had seen a raven only once before on a trip to Montana. At first, I believed it to be a very large crow—and perhaps it was—but there it was on the telephone wire outside my office, calling down at me.

I'd had a new client that day, a pleasant woman who had just arrived from Taos, New Mexico. As we talked, she painted a picture of the dessert in bloom, green mountains, and friendly people.

She sought me out because she was extremely depressed. A serious illness caused her to leave the land she had come to love. Ten years ago with a sleeping bag, a couple changes of clothes, and little money, she had driven away from Rhode Island and an abusive marriage and off into the horizon with no destination in mind, only the need to get as far away from the hurt as possible. She said she would never forget coming through the mountains, making a left hand turn and seeing the town of Taos, New Mexico ahead of her, feeling that finally she had returned home.

Later that afternoon, going over my notes from our session, I wondered about New Mexico. Where was it exactly? I got out my atlas and found it between Texas and Arizona. Waiting for my next client I searched Taos, New Mexico on the Internet and had to admit it looked like an interesting place. Tumbleweed and sage in most areas and glorious rock formations in colors of the sunset. The town of Taos itself was nestled in a valley between green mountains. *Nice place*, I thought and closed down my computer for the night.

When I reached my apartment building, I was irritated to find a large pick-up truck had parked in front of the driveway. I sat there for a moment looking at the unfamiliar truck wondering how long he intended to park there. I first noticed the license plate . . . New Mexico . . . and then the decal in the window saying "Visit Taos." I chuckled to myself about this strange coincidence and drove around the block hoping the vehicle would be gone when I returned and it was.

The next day my friend and fellow shamanic healer called to see if I would be traveling to Peru again this year with her and her husband.

"No, June, I think I'm supposed to go to New Mexico."

"Oh, really," she said, and started to laugh.

"Really," I said. "I think I'm being called to New Mexico."

"Well, I think you are too," she said, "because Jose wanted me to ask you to be the cook on one of his expeditions to Arizona."

"Well, that's right next to New Mexico," I said, and she laughed again.

"Linda," she started, "the other cook on the expedition is none other that Lesley from the shamanic apprenticeship program we took four years ago. She's moved to Taos, New Mexico."

"Yes, I'll go . . . definitely," I told her and wondered what this was all about.

I called Lesley the next day and she invited me to come early and stay with her for a week before we drove on to Arizona and the camping expedition. I was excited to see what New Mexico and Arizona had in store for me.

Travel plans were made, everything fell into place, and the first week of July found me driving in a rental car I'd picked up in Albuquerque down the same road my client had so many years earlier. Although I was exhausted from the flights out with the usual delays, I rolled down the windows and felt totally free. A heavenly scent filled the car and I breathed it in deeply. Soon, my brain identified the wonderful aroma as sage and pine. Those scrubby gray-green bushes must be sagebrush . . . and the little pines, the famous pinions that pine nuts come from. At that moment, my daydream of a cowboy riding out of the sunset to carry me away on his horse didn't seem ridiculous at all.

It was a long drive and I was starting to question whether I'd make Taos before dark. Here I was in a very strange land with no street lights and many dark shapes as the sun sank quickly behind the canyon walls. Just when I was feeling apprehensive about the sheer drops, no guardrails, and my questionable night vision, I saw the twinkling lights of Taos in the distance. I breathed a sigh of relief. I would make it after all. I called Lesley on my cell phone and she met me on the outskirts of town.

I followed Lesley to her beautiful little adobe home, and after some catching up over a hot cup of tea, fell into a deep sleep. When I woke late in the morning she was gone and I found a note telling me to make myself at home and she'd return around noon.

Barefoot, I poured myself a big mug of steaming coffee and went outside to explore the yard and breathe in the sage and pine. There from her patio, I sat and gazed at Taos Mountain in the distance. I had to pinch myself to make sure I was really here. When Lesley came home I was still gazing at the mountain with a huge grin on my face. "Yep," she laughed, "you've caught the fever. It's a hard place to leave."

Lesley is the essence of joy and to be around her makes you grin and feel like you're ten years old again. She's someone with whom you can totally be yourself. We flowed together perfectly. An artist and freelance writer, she'd run off to do a job here or there and I would relax, explore the plaza, or find something interesting to do until she returned home. One day I ventured into the field behind the house and picked apples from an old orchard, long abandoned. We ate applesauce with every meal for the rest of the week.

It was a time for me to gently look into and accept the passing of my mother, to let my body heal from the stress and pain which it held.

On Friday night, Lesley told me we were going to get up early the next morning and drive to Abique where her friend Jan—another artist—lived.

"I know you're meant to meet her," she said. "Remember telling me about the little pipe-shaped piece of wood that had been presented to you before you left Rhode Island? Jan is a Pipe Carrier. She studied with a Hopi medicine man for 15 years and has built a kiva on her property where she does ceremony."

Not knowing what the pipe ceremony entailed, but having close ties to Native American tribes of the East, I was sure I'd find it fascinating and be happy to learn about the significance of the medicine pipe.

It rained during the night and Jan called Saturday morning to warn us about the arroyos: little stream beds, normally dry, that during rainy times could flood and wash a car away. Determined to go, we told her we were sure the rain would stop and we'd get as far as we could.

The driveway to Jan's house was two miles of red dirt, which turned into slippery mud when it rained. As we progressed, and the day progressed, Jan would call and tell us the state of the road. Lesley was sure her little four-wheel drive Outback would get us there. We came to the arroyo, I held my breath, and Lesley drove steadily forward, skidding a little but successfully getting us up the other side.

Up ahead in the distance, we saw Jan's beautiful adobe house with a sky blue pick-up truck parked outside. The sun just starting to peak through the clouds reflected off the smooth red walls, turning it to a rich gold. We parked and walked up the path through sunflowers and sage, eager to see Jan. After hugs, she showed us the beautiful home she'd designed that honored each of the four directions. Spectacular views loomed from every window. I was mesmerized. Living on the edge, as it's called, is a challenge, but Jan felt her 52 acres of heaven made it worth any inconvenience.

Jan was packing up her truck to go to an art festival, but she gave us lunch and then took us to the kiva for a pipe ceremony. The kiva, like a tiny whitewashed womb in the Earth, felt very sacred and Jan's ceremony was beautiful and healing. I had asked the four directions to bring magic and motivation to my life once again. With the ceremony ended and the sun starting to drop behind the red rocks, we hugged and left Jan to finish packing her artwork into the old truck. Tomorrow, Lesley and I would head out to Arizona to be camp cooks.

I was up and packed early. I went to sit in the sun while Lesley finished gathering together what she needed for the trip. Looking up at the bright blue sky, I noticed a raven fly in and circle once overhead. Then another raven flew in . . . and another and another and another.

One at a time, each entered the circle until there were twenty or more ravens flying three abreast and then, as I stared, some shifted direction in the circle and began weaving in and out in a perfect Celtic knot. Not sure if I had gone totally insane, I called for Lesley to come and witness what I was seeing. We both stared in amazement at the large black birds, silently flying in formation. We grabbed hands, staring up, wondering what it could mean. And then, one by one, the ravens each left the circle until one lone bird flew the circle overhead and was gone.

We hugged each other, just knowing that the week ahead would be full of magic. We jumped into the car and made our way to meet our friends in Arizona.

It felt good to be on Navaho land—almost like being home. We stopped at a flea market, where I bought a beautiful little corn maiden fetish to bring along with me. We met the other shamanic healers who had traveled from other parts of the country at the entrance to Canyon De Chelly, transferred our gear to trucks, and watched as the others started off to hike down the canyon walls.

Being the official cooks, food handlers certification in our pockets, Lesley and I were blessed to ride with the supplies in the truck driven by our Navaho guide. We bounced over rocks and splashed through rushing water that sometimes came up to the wheel wells. It was wonderful. The land we were traveling to, Black Canyon, had been owned by this particular Navaho family forever and was very sacred. The Anasazi cave dwellers had once called this canyon home. It would be a great honor to camp, do ceremony, and hike this land.

The others arrived just before the rain. Lesley, the guides, and I had used tarps to make a shelter for the food and camp stove. We did our best to get a meal on the table that night. Everyone was so hungry from the hike that they didn't complain.

The next morning, everyone left on a hike except a young man who had hurt his leg the day before, two of the Navaho women, and me. It was Lesley's turn to hike and I'd be in charge of getting lunch ready for the hungry hikers when they returned. I quickly cleaned up the breakfast dishes and started in on the lunch. I worked quickly; in little over an hour, I'd prepared everything necessary. The young man had gone to the other side of the canyon to play his flute and I sat near an old, split rail fence to meditate. I connected to Mother Earth as I always do and expanded my energy out to become one with the Universe. In the distance, I could hear the soft melody of the native flute. Soon I opened my eyes to the crackling of a raven walking back and forth on the fence before me. Once he got my attention, he flew away. I closed my eyes again. Soon in my mediation, I heard someone calling me.

"Here, over here! We are here . . . come, come."

I opened my eyes and looked to my left, over the fence, and to the opposite side of the canyon. It was far away and I could only see that there were some sort of large green plants along the canyon wall. I found the guide and asked if I could cross over the barbed wire and go to the other side of the canyon. She acknowledged me with a smile and went back to her beading. I climbed carefully between the barbed wire and walked through the field. I was almost at the opposite side of the canyon when I head another call.

"Over here, over here sister! We're over here."

Was it the wind? I turned left again and walked around a large rock formation. There it was: a large grouping of jimson weed, my power spirit medicine plant. I admired them when, ever so slightly, they parted so that I saw a small cave behind them. I climbed through the tiny opening and up the narrow passageway to a round room. I turned around and sat facing the mouth of the cave and realized that I had climbed up what appeared to be a birth canal and into a womb. There was an opening at the top, far above my head. The sun hitting the wall of the cave turned it red.

I closed my eyes, leaned against the wall of the womb, and was engulfed with the feeling of love. I felt like that tiny baby, safe once again, in my mother's womb. I felt the love my mother had for me when I had been conceived and the love she has given to me every day, even now that she has passed. I wept silent tears, tears that were unable to be released until now. I gave my tears and pain and sorrow back to Mother Earth, and she embraced and loved me as my own mother had. I was deep in this warm, flowing embrace of loving energy when I heard a distant voice calling my name. I climbed out of the cave after leaving tobacco as an offering and ran back across the field to find my Navaho friend looking worried.

"We didn't see you. Where did you go?"

I told her how the raven had come to get me and that the jimson weed had called to me from across the canyon. I told her of the sacred cave and she put her fingers to her lips.

"Ssshhh," she whispered. "The others will not find it and only those who have been called by the raven are meant to know its secret."

I prepared lunch for my fellow healers. They ate ravenously and we all went to our tents to take a nap. There outside the door of my little tent was the feather of a raven. A sacred gift I will treasure always.

My spirit renewed, I returned to Rhode Island and my healing center. Walking up the drive I was startled to see five ravens sitting on the telephone line waiting for me. They stayed for three days and then disappeared. We have crows in New England, but not so many ravens. Just now, while putting my book together in its final form, I got up to stretch and looked out the window to see what I thought was a group of wild turkeys (common in New England). Putting my glasses on to get a closer look, I was startled to see five ravens walking around under my window. Memories of being held in the womb of Mother Earth came flooding back. I felt her hug and smiled.

Thank you, ravens, for putting your magical touch on my book.

Seeking Sanctuary

I did not wish to live what was not life, living is so dear; nor did I wish to practice resignation, unless it was quite necessary. I wanted to live deep and suck out all the marrow of life . . .
Henry David Thoreau

For months, I had been searching the Internet and real estate papers for the perfect property. My feelings of wanting to escape to a quieter place and time were becoming an obsession. I knew I wanted to run away from everything bringing me unhappiness; at this point in my life, I questioned if I had ever been happy. I was tired of trying to hold everything together. Outwardly, it was becoming more and more difficult to hide the fact to my clients and friends that this healer was in need of healing. It is hard to be the bright, uplifting spirit called upon to work successfully with the chronically ill if you yourself feel like your soul has died.

I had burned out and didn't even recognize the signs or cause. I thought I was still grieving the death of my mother a year earlier. I was; but on top of that, I was trying to hold together a business that put restrictions on me and took away my freedom. The harder I worked at trying to hold it together, the more it fell apart.

In my wanting to run away, I held a very clear vision of what the perfect refuge would look like and this is the property I searched for. If I could just be alone with Mother Earth, I knew I would heal or make sense of those alone places deep in my heart.

Enlisting the company of a friend, I even drove to West Virginia to check out a little cabin on 26 acres on the top of a mountain. The trip was an adventure, but this definitely wasn't the place I had dreamed about. It did help me clarify how "away from it all" I really wanted to be. Maybe not as far as I had thought, I realized.

I kept the vision of my sanctuary in my mind, knowing that someday it would present itself. I envisioned purchasing this property, but Spirit works in mysterious and usually very beneficial ways, often giving us just what we need, rather than what we have asked for.

One day, I decided to search the Internet for house-sitting assignments. My friend Gary had just returned from spending a week on the shore taking care of a lovely house and couple of dogs. Curious to see if there was actually a website for this sort of thing, I did an Internet search. To my surprise, there were actually websites devoted to this.

I clicked on the first one and a list of house-sitting opportunities all over the world popped up. I scanned the list and noticed one in Jackson, New Hampshire for the month of September. Familiar with the town of Jackson, and knowing that September was the most perfect month to be in the White Mountains, I felt shivers up and down my body and knew this would be the perfect place to recover from what had been an extremely stressful year. I paid my fee to the site and sent an e-mail off to the property owners.

After we corresponded back and forth a couple of times, I drove the four hours to meet with them. It truly was a match made in heaven. Sam and Betsy's home was lovely and spacious, sitting on 15 acres in a field of wildflowers, nestled in the woods. My only duty was to lovingly care for their dog, Carter: a happy, bouncy Labradoodle.

He had the intelligence of a poodle and the loving, laid-back personality of a Lab. It was love at first sight for the pooch and me. The home owners welcomed me and I felt at home and with dear friends from the moment we greeted each other.

I returned to the city to prepare for my stay in the mountains. The weekend away was enough for me to decide that I could no longer continue to operate a business that my heart was no longer in. I gave notice to my landlord and office mate and packed my belongings. I immediately started to feel lighter and happier.

Determined to release what no longer serves me, I trust that Spirit will not let me down.

Transformation

I have calmed and quieted my soul . . . like a child quieted is my soul.
Psalms 13:1–2

Once a caterpillar feasts on milkweed, it feels the call to close in upon itself.

Sam and Betsy discovered it already within a crystalline shell of its own making. A place to hide away from the world, a place to dissolve the old and begin to create the new.

I was entrusted with its care while they traveled and I carried it to a safe, sheltered place where I could watch its progress.

Every day transformation was taking place within the iridescent cocoon. Each day as I examined it, I could see changes taking place. Finally the distinct orange and black of the monarch showed within the tiny capsule. Five days later the tiny shell had been broken through and a beautiful full grown butterfly was sitting in its place. Wings still wet, it sat with me for hours.

I watched as the butterfly tentatively opened its wings. It did this slowly a few times and then turned its head from side to side as I do after a long night's sleep to get the kinks out. It raised first one leg, then another, until all four had been stretched. Then it rested. Ten minutes later, it started the same routine again. Spreading its wings a little further each time, it performed its opening-and-closing exercise for a longer stretch. I watched closely and saw the tension and slight vibration as it opened and closed, opened and closed until the butterfly was tired. Then it rested for another ten minutes.

I could see that this was not an easy task for the little creature, but took real determination. Once again, it opened and closed its wings, turned its head from side to side, side to side, and did leg lifts. This time the tightly closed proboscis was slowly unfurled part way, then another try and it fully extended. Soon it would taste the sweetness that life had in store for it. This routine went on for another half hour until finally, quivering and vibrating its wings, it rose into the sky. I said good-bye and wished it well on its journey.

The bright new butterfly flew in a circle overhead and then dropped to the ground after a brief flight. After a few minutes it took off again and flew to my arm. I was filled with amazement and love for this delicate little creature I had shared the past hours with, thankful for its message to me that transformation is not instantaneous and it's okay to rest until you're truly ready to fly. Eye-to-eye, I said my good-byes again and the butterfly's wings, stronger this time, lifted it off and over the tree tops.

I sat in the silence of nature wondering how anyone who had witnessed the birth of a butterfly could not believe in God or miracles. What else would you call a tiny delicate creature standing on legs as fine as thread, balancing heavy wings, each delicate brush stroke painted by the hands of God clearly visible.

Here I am in my self-chosen cocoon in the mountains. I vow to be patient with myself, to rest when needed, to sit and just be . . . until, like the beautiful butterfly, I determine from some inner knowing that it's time to try my wings. I know that it may take several tries before I truly have the strength and courage to lift myself over the tree tops to what awaits me, for I too am a miracle.

Plunging in Over My Head

Here in this body are the sacred rivers: Here are the sun and moon, as
well as the pilgrimage places.
I have not encountered another temple as blissful as my own body.
Saraha

Like the butterfly, this has been a *slow* process. I'd like to say I've been meditating for hours at a time—not so. There is underlying anxiety most of the time, with brief hours of peace . . . soul peace, I'm talking about. The surroundings are incredibly peaceful here, but internally I'm not.

Yesterday, I walked down to the river and instead of wishing the water was warmer, or the air was warmer, or I'd brought my bathing suit, I quit making excuses, shed my clothes and waded into the freezing water. If I could get past the hard places—the slippery river stones—I could get to the deep water and dive in. I inched my way gingerly into the COLD water, refreshing after I'd submerged each body part for awhile.

I finally got up to my hips and stood there in the strong current taking an extraordinarily long time deciding to take the plunge. My body was saying, *Hey, you've gone far enough, it will be really cold.* Another voice, my mind, was saying, *Think of the wonderful feeling of freedom you'll have.* And then in the background of the voices, I heard my long-silent Wild Woman spirit chiding, "Wow . . . you've really lost your sense of adventure. Who are you, anyway?"

Gingerly, I splashed the icy water on my arms, chest, and back—and silently asked angels for a push. Yikes! Wow! Incredible! I was screaming and laughing, swimming above the deep dark pothole. I looked up at the huge boulder beside me that I thought of as a secure place to grab onto when I noticed a huge, dangerous looking spider staring down at me. This was *his* territory, so I pushed off again into the deep water.

The current was strong, but with great effort, I could swim upstream a little and then let the current carry me down on my back. I felt weightless like a leaf and noted how I wasn't really dashed into any rocks, but was eased around them if I didn't fight the current. With the water silencing my ears and my eyes open to the blue sky and colored leaves above, I found myself in another world. I felt the years slip away, and those childlike feelings come back. I let the current take me out of the deep water and gently float me back to shore.

Unselfconsciously, I stood up and walked upstream to another pothole where I dove in to play for another ten minutes before returning to shore. I climbed out and watched my companion Carter, the Labradoodle, give himself a good shake. I, too, gave myself a good shake sending cares, anxiety and stress flying in all directions.

I shouted a loud thank you to the sky and vowed to remember what Mother had taught me today.

If I walk consciously through the hard places to the deep unknown with trust and no resistance, I will be carried safely to a place of greater peace and delight.

Release and Trust

*Father, Mother, God, Goddess, Spirit of All There Is, thank you for
blessing me this day with your vision and love. Thank you for embracing
me and supporting me as I travel on this journey of my soul.*
Linda Hogan, author & believer

It's February 27th and I'm on retreat again. I know my life is
blessed. Coming back to Sam and Betsy's house is like returning
home. Who would have thought answering a house sitting ad would
lead to a wonderful friendship and opportunity to periodically renew
my spirit within the arms of Mother Nature.

I left the city frustrated, tired, and drained. A recent astrological
reading foretold of many more days of feeling tired and alone with
many life determining decisions to make in the upcoming months.

January had given me a brief respite and I believed that with the
new year my passion and purpose would return. This latest
information was not what I was expecting nor looking for.

As soon as mountains came into view, I started to relax and feel
my spirits lift and before I knew it I was in Jackson, once again, with
Carter, my favorite dog. He's a wonderful companion and I briefly
pondered whether I should get my own dog. No, for now, Carter
would be my part-time pooch. It's hard enough to travel and leave my
independent kitty, Luna. For now, I will pass on a canine companion.

By the next morning, my friends had left for Montreal, and Carter and I were alone. I grabbed Betsy's snowshoes and we headed out to the field. Carter frolicked in the snow and I trudged along finding it hard going. This out of shape body was getting a real workout as I marched through the deep snow. I finally collapsed in a snow drift with my eyes closed wondering if I would ever get my life back in order. Would I make the correct decisions to head my life off in the right direction or would I continue to hold on to that which was holding me back. Could I ever freely let go of the old to make way for the new? Once I had been fearless—but now, I was just tired.

"You're tired from holding on so tightly," was what I heard a voice deep within say. "You don't need to carry the burden any longer, just release it to me."

I opened my eyes and looked up at the deep blue sky. There, staring back at me, was a beautiful face both feminine and masculine at the same time. I felt a great peace come over me as I felt myself being embraced by the Mother-Father Spirit that I call upon when I do my healing work or pray. I gazed upon the beauty of this wise face with the feminine eyes and strong masculine nose and mouth and felt comforted.

"Yes, I believe with your help I can release the fear and the feelings that are holding me prisoner," I whispered back to the sky.

Once again, the Earth and Universe has given me solace. I know as long as I stay connected, I will move forward with a free heart and spirit, and I will be placed exactly where I need to be.

Our True Essence Is Love and Beauty

Signs sent from above affirm that love lives on.
Roland M. Comtois, *And Then There Was Heaven*

Here I lie on my bed, numb, void of feelings, and totally exhausted. It has been a long, hard year holding the hand of one of my best friends as she gracefully went through cancer and a painful death, painful for me and those who loved her. I choose to stick to my belief that her spirit had left her body long before these last heart wrenching days.

My body feels too heavy to move as I lie on the bed waiting to dress and drive to her wake. I argue with myself as I keep getting the message to get up and go out into the sunshine and sit in the park across the street. I really don't want to. I'm too exhausted. I just don't want to make the effort. Please just let me have some peace I whisper to the empty room. No! Get up and go to the park now!

Finally succumbing to the insistent nagging of my mind, I slip on shoes, grab a sweater, and woodenly walk out the door, down the stairs and across to the park. It's quiet at this time of day and I sit under the big pine tree where I sometimes meditate. The sun shines upon me and I feel embraced and loved by the tree. I haven't been able to shed tears for myself yet. I'd already shed many for my friend as her disease progressed, taking away more and more of her freedom each day. My only emotions seemed to be anger and rage at the injustice of disease and death coming to such a vibrant, beautiful, compassionate, spiritual woman. "I don't understand" seemed to be the only affirmation coming from my lips these days.

Sitting on the Earth leaning against the big pine, I plead for some relief from the tension coursing through my body. Shoulders up around my ears and fingers clenched into tight fists I want to scream or fight. I make myself take a deep breath and then another. I start to relax and find comfort as I'm supported by the tree. Relaxing my fingers I let them scratch into the Earth near the roots of the pine and the musky scent of Mother Earth wafts upward and engulfs me. I feel some sense of peace and recognition of home. I sit quietly watching the leaves turned gold in the sun rustling with the breeze. Occasionally one breaks free and floats or spins toward Earth.

It is in this peace that I feel my friend Cat sitting beside me shoulder to shoulder, head to head as we often did while reading a book or watching a movie. I sigh and just enjoy her presence. As I sit looking at the park from my spot by the tree my senses are opened and once again everything I gaze upon is beautiful. I can feel her in the wind, smell her in the Earth, and see her in the clouds and blue of the sky. It's as though I'm sitting with her once again as we had so many times before her illness, two little girls totally in awe of the beauty of the Earth and God. I can see her essence in everything. Feeling her freedom, I smile.

As I get up to leave, I hear her say, "No, look over here." Looking to the spot where her spirit had rested with me, I see some low growing green weeds. I pick two stems and hold them to my eyes.

Barely visible tucked among the leaves are tiny white flowers with a yellow center.

"Daisies for fairies," I murmur.

Then I hear Cat—somewhere in my heart—say, "Remember Linda, there is beauty in every day and in every situation. Sometimes it's just really hard to see, but if you search for awhile, you will always find it."

Thank you, Cat, my dear sweet friend, for sharing so many magic moments with me. Thank you for letting me know that you are still with me in my heart and I will see you in the glorious beauty of the Earth and Sky.

Whispers From Gentle Breeze

The most beautiful thing we can experience is the mysterious. It is the source of all true art and all science. He to whom this emotion is a stranger, who can no longer pause to wonder and stand rapt in awe, is as good as dead! His eyes are closed.
Albert Einstein

Three spring-like days in a row in the middle of January are reason to celebrate.

I woke early and caught up on e-mail and prepared for the class on manifesting that I'll be teaching tonight. I always like to recharge myself before teaching others and the Monastery is my favorite place. Running out the door with a clean face and hiking boots, I nearly tumble over a fluffy white dog, with a foreign name I can never remember, on a leash with his dog walker. He's the cutest little mop of a dog and I snuggle him a moment before heading off.

I love dogs and often dream of having one, but Luna, my independent kitty, is much more appropriate for someone who looks for any excuse to travel and takes off for weeks at a time. Fortunately for Luna, and because of her winning personality, there are always friends or neighbors ready to feed and love her.

I enjoy my ride to Cumberland. I sight a number of hawks sitting in trees along the highway and know it will be an interesting day. Hawks always mean watch for a message from Spirit. Sometimes it can be an affirmation of what I'm thinking about; but today, I feel I'll get my message in the woods.

Pulling into the drive, I turn left instead of right. I usually park and walk counterclockwise around the old grounds for no particular reason other than habit. It's the first place I parked after discovering this wonderland and it's just part of my routine. It's the beginning of a new year and if you want change in your life, they say, you have to be the change. So, today I park by the left entrance to the trail and wonder how I'll view the woods from this different angle.

Stepping onto the shaded path, taking a deep breath and thanking spirit for this beautiful day, I am immediately gifted with the scent of juniper. My nose lifts to the sky and my ears perk up. More than once I've been likened to a bear coming out of hibernation. I thank God for my nose and ability to hone right in on the most indistinguishable scents. I know this talent comes from having consciously connected to the Earth for so long. All of my senses have been heightened and I often smell, hear and see what others are oblivious to. In this moment I'm totally glad to be me.

I stride down the trail trying to burn a few calories. Normally I walk in a trance-like state, oooing and ahhing at a new leaf here or an ice crystal there. I totally lose myself when I'm in the woods and time flies by without my noticing. Teaching class tonight, I know I can't linger as long as I'd like and decide to stay on the marked trail making the full loop while enjoying all there is to see and smell. There will be no detours today!

Before I know it, I'm off the trail and into the woods (but just for a short way, I tell myself). I'll take a quick sit in the sunny field when I get back to the car. Here's my favorite rock. How can I pass it by? I can't and find myself hugging the big boulder that looks like the giant head of a troll. Then I'm sitting on the little stone at the base of the tree where I come to mediate and it feels wonderful as the tree molds to my well known body. Ah, I'm home again and the peace is so heavenly.

I connect to the Earth and fill myself with her generously offered energy. Then I ask God to use me as a conduit to return the healing energy of Universal Love back to her. I sit in this symbiotic embrace for awhile until I sense a presence near me. I open my eyes and not seeing anyone with two legs or four, ask that they show themselves.

The dried golden leaves that the beech trees refuse to part with start to rustle. Is that you Grandfather Wind, I ask out loud? To my right, under the beeches, I notice an eternal figure. In my mind I hear a whispering voice. The kind of voice your girlfriend might use when sharing secrets.

No, it's not Grandfather, it's me, Gentle Breeze, one of his granddaughters. From the side of my vision, in my mind's eye I see her take form. I remember hearing my father talk about his cousin who was a "wisp of a girl." Now I know what he meant. This vision radiating in pale blue energy is thin and delicate and moves her arms gracefully as she talks. She is beautiful, almost as if your breath on a cold day has taken the form of a delicate young woman. I just sit enjoying her presence. I've learned to keep my thoughts to myself on these occasions and just listen.

Her words astounded me. *We want to tell you how graceful you are*, she breathed. I almost scream out loud, "Are you kidding?!"

Her laughter, like the sound of two crystal goblets hitting together, brings me back to my former high vibration.

Yes, you walk gently upon this Earth, she whispers. *Have you ever fallen or tripped, or stepped on a flower or bug while in the woods? No! Whether you're climbing a mountain, walking on a beach or hiking in the woods, you are always sure footed and gentle on the land. Mother says you do not do well with hard surfaces because you're too bouncy. There is no give to blacktop and cement and your sharp edged furniture and floors. Your vibration is that of the wind. Your spirit wants to pass through and over things but your body is still solid. For now, that's the way it must be. Know that in our realm you are thought of as a gentle and graceful spirit of the Earth.*

And then, message given, she is gone.

Leaning against the tree for awhile, I marvel at my life and how blessed I am to be so connected to nature and her spirits. It brings to mind my friend Cat who recently passed on to another realm. She was the girlfriend I whispered secrets with, the friend who would call me up to look out the window to see the pink clouds. When I'm still and out in nature, I can still feel her presence and hear her words. I like to believe that she's the one painting sunsets or teaching baby birds to sing. When it's my time to transform into a being of spirit, I, too, will have some hand in adding to Mother Nature's glory.

For now, like a gentle breeze, I will try to flow gently through life, in and around people teaching them to walk gently upon the Earth.

Living Art

Nature is the Art of God.
Thomas Browne

Carter nudges me and I finally get out of bed on this beautiful September morning. Once again I've been blessed to stay with my favorite pooch while his wonderful owners travel. He waits patiently while I make myself some coffee and toast and sit out on the deck to gaze at Carter Notch in the early morning sunlight. The wind blows clouds across the sun making the mountain seem to dance.

I breathe in the fresh crisp air and I'm as eager as Carter to take my first walk down to the river after having been gone for six months.

Things change little up here in the mountains; but as I walk down the mowed path through the field to the river, I see that this year Lucy and Dexter—self-appointed stewards of this land—have let the milkweed grow up for the monarch butterflies. It is still early, but a few soar among the purple asters and goldenrod searching for just the perfect tasty morsel. Most are still wrapped tightly in cocoons waiting for the perfect moment to burst out. Dexter and Lucy could have weeded out the milkweed a few years ago and continued to sell the hay. However, because they are what I like to call Earth Angels, they let it flourish (much to the dismay of local farmers) so that the habitat of the monarch butterfly would be spared. Each time I see an orange and black butterfly, no matter where I am, I will think of them and silently thank them.

Carter leaps ahead of me and I follow him to the edge of the field and onto the woods path. The dappled woods are dark and moist. I send greetings to a grandfather of a log covered in bright green moss like velvet. Some day at dusk I will come with my camera to seek out fairies. If I were a fairy, I would certainly be dancing on this log.

Carter barks for me. He has run ahead to the river and is waiting with a stick in his mouth for the fun to begin. I toss it a few times for him and then settle on a large stone at the edge of the water. As I sit facing upstream and gaze at the shallow water rushing past, I marvel at how today the sunlight hitting the water catches the current and forms a reptilian pattern on the rocks beneath. I have an alligator bag given to me by a dear friend; this gold-and-black pattern flowing over the rocks looks exactly the same. As I continue to stare at the water, I see that there are black dots, of many different sizes, encircled in golden light, also flowing along. I look above, thinking perhaps it's clouds—but the sky is clear. Could it be pollution of some kind? I stick my hand into the water and let it flow across my palm. There is no residue or smell. I have never seen anything like this here and it is a little unsettling—yet, I know I have seen them somewhere. Yes! They look and move exactly like the red blood cells of live blood. Could I be seeing the living essence and life force of this river? I choose to believe this and send a prayer of gratitude and healing to the water flowing past.

When I return later to swim, this pattern of light will have changed. It was a beautiful piece of art created for a moment and continually changing. How could any artwork by the greatest artists of the world compare to this? Nature is the most profound multimedia event that you will ever experience. Why not turn off your television and go witness the greatest show on Earth.

The Emerald River

A wise man is he who does not grieve for the things which he has not, but rejoices for those which he has.
Epictetus, Greek philosopher

10:18 AM: I push play and retrieve missed messages.

"Sorry I didn't call back the other day. I'm very busy."

Busy. Business, all business, always business.

I expected more.

"It's never enough," he says. Yes, it's never enough.

I wrap a heavy shroud of mixed feelings—none of them good—around my body and go off to accomplish what I'd planned for the day. Oblivious to the world, I drive over the mountain to pick up fresh eggs from the farm, take trash to the transfer station, and stop at the store for juice and a chocolate bar. Once again, I'm in New Hampshire taking care of my favorite pooch.

Carter sits quietly in the back seat. He can read the energy flowing off of me and doesn't like it.

3:33 PM: I look at the grandfather clock in the hallway. I stop momentarily, recognizing that 333 is a magic number for me. I pick up the leash and call Carter. He pounces and bounces, ecstatically racing toward the door. We reach the field and I unhook his leash and let him run ahead to the river. I don't feel like running today, and walk along feeling like I have weights in my shoes. I notice that part of the field has been mowed. The milkweed has been left until the last monarch butterflies have burst from their cocoons. I smile and think of Lucy and Dexter and the difference they're making in the world.

I reach the river where I find Carter happily chewing up a stick that he has salvaged from the rushing water. I find a rock in the sun, take off my shoes and socks, and stick my toes into the icy water. A school of tiny fish, perhaps trout, darts at my toes curiously. I watch as more and more silver darts of light play a game with my feet. I can't help but laugh.

I close my eyes and give thanks for the beautiful day and all the blessings that are mine. I sit feeling the sun on the top of my head and the slight breeze that blows my hair. I open my eyes and look back at the river and the flowing water has turned emerald green. Sun hitting the leaves reflects back into the water and it shimmers and flows the color of emeralds, clear and brilliant. The stones at the edge of the water have turned a deep blue. I stare and take the scene in. My mind tries to rationalize blue stones, suggesting perhaps it is the reflection of the sky.

I sometimes question whether others would see the same things I see if they were still long enough. I do know that while I was lost in dark emotions, none of this was visible to me. When I relaxed and gave thanks and existed in a new moment, all this beauty became apparent.

I snap on Carter's leash and head back to the house. Individual blades of brilliant green grass made up the path and I saw intricate patterns in the leaves and wild flowers. I let myself soak up the healing green energy being presented to me and vow to let the past be the past. I know the blue stones are to remind me of the importance of communication.

Once again, Mother Earth has opened my eyes to what is really important: to love for the sake of loving, to recognize the love that is offered from all sources, to be grateful for that which is, and to ignore that which isn't.

Soaking Up the Being

And this, our life, exempt from public haunt, finds tongues in trees, books in the running brook, sermons in stones, and good in everything.
William Shakespeare, *As You Like It*

My friend Gary, who has become surrogate roommate to my cat Luna in my absence, called this morning and suggested that I soak up all the "Being" (as in "To Just Be") that I can today before I return home.

"I plan on doing just that," I told him. "I've finished mowing the lawns, tidied up the house, have my rubber sandals on, and I'm heading to the river as we speak. It is going to be a glorious day and I intend to sit and Be for as long as Spirit moves me."

Overnight, the leaves of maples and oaks have changed to reds and oranges and the birches to yellow. Crawford's Notch wears a different dress this morning as Carter and I head across the field, completely mown now that the monarchs have moved on.

I'm surprised when I get to the river to see that the water has risen at least three feet. It now flows over the top of the small dam made earlier in the season by some neighbors wishing for a deeper swimming hole. It's plenty deep in the channel now, but the gently flowing water is much too cold for me. The Earth is dry and we haven't had rain for several weeks. Perhaps it has rained high up in the mountains or some snow pockets have melted because of the unseasonably warm weather. Eighty-five degrees on a late September morning is unusual here in New Hampshire.

The stone I sat upon when I first arrived for my retreat a few weeks ago is submerged under water. A boulder I usually sit on at the edge of the river is now surrounded by the icy water, but I wade in up to my knees, glad that I've put on my river shoes. I reach the boulder and pull myself up in the sun. Carter thinks it's great fun and races around and around the rock splashing and getting me wet. I can't help but laugh at his antics. He's the happiest dog I know and is a wonderful companion. I ignore him and he goes off to entertain himself by chasing leaves that fall into the river and move downstream.

I connect to the Earth through the warm stone I'm perched upon and feel her energy rise through my body. Now I'm as warm on the inside as on the outside. It's a good feeling. Eyes closed, I sit on the rock and "just be." The air is balmy and although I have never seen a gossamer blanket, I know exactly what it would feel like as a slight breeze swirls around me. I sit facing the north; the smell of dry and decaying leaves fills my nostrils.

I turn my head slightly to the east. The fragrance of pine and balsam wash over me, reminding me of the balsam pillow bought for me by my parents so many years ago on a trip to the White Mountains. My parents are now both gone, as well as the family home, but the pillow rests beside my bed in the city. When I shake it, a faint smell of the forests . . . and home . . . still remains.

I smell something sweet. I turn my head to hone in on the scent and discover it is from hay drying in the field beyond the woods. My friends make fun of my sense of smell. I've been likened to a bear as I stand, head tilted back, nose to the wind breathing deeply.

Oh, I am so blessed to be able to smell the Earth and her heavenly fragrances.

Bluebell

Do you believe in fairies? Say quick that you believe. If you believe, clap your hands!
James M. Barrie

O Glorious Day! What a wonderful life to wake up to the possibility of magic and miracles every morning.

Last night, being the full moon, Hunters Moon, or Harvest Moon (depending on where in New England you happen to be), I decided to leave sweets on the moss covered boulder at the edge of the forest with hope that I would entice fairies to this place and capture them in photos. Usually, before trying to make contact with any of Mother Earth's creatures, seen or unseen, I frequent the area often and sit quietly, sometimes leaving gifts or singing a song.

I had been in this area, but only while mowing the lawn, having rested here in the shade on a few occasions. But this was the night of the full moon and sometimes the veil is thinner then. It certainly was a magical night as the big yellow moon rose above the majestic pine trees casting a soft glow over the field and yard. I set an opened Oreo cookie on the rock and sprinkled sugar all around. I whispered an invitation to the fairies I hoped watched me from the woods and left.

At midnight, I gathered up my digital camera and left the house. Silently, I walked to the boulder where I had prepared the fairy feast. Seeing nothing with my naked eye, I held up the camera and shot a photo into the dark. There, captured on the screen, were hundreds of tiny little orbs floating above and around the rock. Orbs are the spheres of usually transparent energy, looking very much the soap bubbles blown by a child. I was ecstatic, but decided to shoot more photos to make sure this was not merely a malfunction of the camera.

I walked several feet to another large boulder, aimed my camera and shot again. It showed a very clear picture of the large rock covered in moss and leaves, but no orbs.

I went back and shot photos of the rock where I'd placed the sugar and cookie. Once again, hundreds of little orbs looking like soap bubbles a child might have blown were covering the rock. Not wishing to disturb the festivities, I turned and silently crossed the yard to the flower lined brick walk leading up to the house. I lifted my camera again and captured more fairies on film, not as thickly grouped, but a good number of little orbs among the asters and mums.

Going around to the other side of the flower bed I snapped a picture that revealed nothing. This was definitely something magical, not mechanical. I smiled and went into the house and up to bed.

This morning, I checked my e-mail as usual and the first message was from my friend Krista. She'd sent along photos she'd taken in England of a Bluebell Wood. "It will make the perfect cover for your fairy book," she wrote. I laughed to myself thinking how connected we all are. Last night I'm luring fairies, and this morning my first message from a friend is about a fairy book that I'll write someday.

I let Carter out for his morning run and stood gazing across the yard at the boulder where last night's magic had transpired. I thought to myself how good it was to have the photos secure in my camera.

Most people would think I'm crazy. Sometimes, I question my own reality, which is so different from the majority of people on this planet. In my reverie, I wondered when I would be connected enough to see a fairy with my naked eye again. It had been two years since the white fairy in my bedroom had asked me to write a book.

I thought about the first tiny fairy in the blue dress that I had seen on only two occasions at my wellness center and wondered if she was still there. I knew she couldn't show herself to the non-believers, but wondered if she was still living there by the river waiting for a child, not yet jaded by the world, to come by. I was thinking how I had called her Lily, wondering if it was her true name . . . when sparkling like a jewel, she flew around the corner of the porch and landed on the front of my shirt.

"You can call me Bluebell," I heard as I stared at her perfect little fairy wings and fluffy light blue dress, the same she'd been wearing years ago when I first met her. My mind raced with questions: "How are you here?" "Isn't your home in Rhode Island by the water?" "Don't devas and nature spirits stay and watch over particular places?"

"I watch over you," she said, and was gone.

Oh, what Joy! I have my own personal fairy . . . just like Peter Pan. It's comforting to know that magic goes along with me wherever I travel. I question my sanity for a moment and laugh. Whether I'm creating my world or tapping into another reality, or just plain nuts, it doesn't really matter. It lights my being from within; hopefully, by sharing this, others may see the light and open their eyes to the magic and miracles of our beautiful Earth, too.

I Know How the Red Tulip Feels

Deep in their roots, all flowers keep the light.
Theodore Roethke, American poet

From our perspective, it's long overdue. Spring, a time of bursting forth into our promised glory, officially began three weeks ago. Ripe with vision, swollen with a knowing that radical change is about to take place, traces of our true colors just starting to show, the red tulip and I wait for what seems like an eternity.

The seeds were planted long ago and we've been growing, fed by Mother Earth and Spirit, for many seasons. Feeling the growth, but not knowing what it was that we were becoming, we sometimes hesitated and chose to remain dormant. But something is different this spring. Our bulbs, now full of potential, have sent before us green shoots determined to push through the cold and finally taste the sun. This year, everything in place and ready for us, we have an inkling of what lies ahead. Unable to contain our true selves any longer, we shout a loud *yes!*

So, here we stand in anticipation, as cold winds blow the last few snowflakes of the year around us. Impatient, yes—but knowing that very soon we will have transformed into the glorious promise of who we are truly meant to be. We will be the gift.

June 5, 2008

A Channeled Message from Mother Earth

It has been a difficult week for many of you, two-legged and four-legged alike. There is a great confusion of energies coming in and leaving the planet at this time.

Many of my creatures are finding themselves where they do not belong. Animals are straying from their normal territories and finding themselves in harm's way.

Time is speeding forward and you are all trying to keep up but it may seem as if you are walking in a fog. Many are unconscious and this can be a dangerous situation. It may seem as if you are wandering in this fog alone; but there are many others there, wandering in their own fog, and you often collide. When you collide there is fear, which turns to anger.

There are many fears surfacing now. Finances and security are the two largest ones. I want to assure you that there is nothing to fear. Everything you need to be sustained, I provide for you. You may see changes in your material world, but only those unnecessary things you've become accustomed to will diminish.

You need to stay conscious and in your bodies at this time. Because of these uncomfortable energies, many subconsciously want to leave the planet as it would seem to be a solution.

It is *not*. Your help is needed here now and in the future days ahead.

You need to come to me daily now to ground and stay centered and awake. Your pace will slow and you will remain peaceful and aware. In this way you will avoid colliding with those in the fog.

You also need to pay attention to water. Go to the water, pray to the water, bathe in and drink the water. Give thanks for water. It will cleanse you and purify you and help you stay awake.

When you feel anxiety or tension connect to me for strength.

Remember: we are One.

June 21, 2008

A Channeled Message from Mother Earth

This evening, I asked some friends to join me at one of my favorite meditation spots on a cliff high above the Atlantic Ocean. I led them through a meditation to honor Mother Earth and acknowledge the solstice.

We stayed connected to her energy in a blissful state for over twenty minutes before opening our eyes. Whenever I teach others to connect to the Earth, I tell them that when they open their eyes they may notice things not normally seen and that everything usually appears brighter and clearer. I smiled to myself and thought of the time I was teaching a student to connect to the Earth and upon opening our eyes we found the fairy Bluebell dancing between us.

This time as we opened our eyes, a bird closely followed or chased by a butterfly flew right through the middle of our circle. We all laughed as our eyes followed the two flying down the path.

I believe Spirit speaks to us through nature and I pay close attention to these signs. When unusual things happen I take them as an omen. A bird being chased by a butterfly is certainly significant.

Birds are said to be prophetic and have always symbolized messengers from Spirit for me. If I see a hawk fly over head, I always believe it is a confirmation of what I've been thinking about. One of my friends identified the bird as a swallow. When I was a little girl the old farmer next door told me that my house was protected because a swallow had chosen to build his house under the eaves of our house. He said it was a good omen.

A butterfly symbolizes transformation and new beginnings. The color yellow is a symbol for optimism and happiness. My interpretation of this omen is that on this solstice, the energy coming in and the conscious work we are doing will herald in a time of protection followed by hope and optimism.

I then asked Mother Earth if she had a message. This was her reply.

Children,

I am proud of you. I know those of you who consciously connect to my energy have felt the pulling and draining as I use your energy to help me transmute fear.

You have not given in to the headaches, backaches, and purging and have gathered in Spirit to help the planet—although it has been uncomfortable for many of you.

You have listened, heard me calling, and taken your places to help. Thank you.

By gathering together the healing is intensified. Continue to gather in the days ahead. Your help will be needed. Gather, connect, and just be. Nothing else is necessary except to hold your beautiful vibration of love.

Remember: we are one.

At Day's End

I will arise and go now, and go to Innisfree,
And a small cabin build there, of clay and wattles made:
Nine bean-rows will I have there, and a hive for the honey-bee;
And live alone in the bee-loud glade.
William Butler Yeats, "The Lake Isle of Innisfree"

Lucy called, spur of the moment, from New Hampshire and asked if I could possibly come and spend the week with Anton (their very old cat) while they traveled.

"Of course," was my response, not hesitating for a moment. Hastily, I rearranged my schedule so I could spend five days basking in nature. I know I am blessed to be able to do this, but I've consciously created my life just for these occasions and feel no guilt.

Two days after the phone call I've arrived and given Anton some loving. I grab a towel and find my way down the path through milkweed, as fragrant as the most highly prized lilies, to the river. Inhaling deeply, I wonder how many others know that this weed with beautiful pink star flower clusters is such a treasure, or do they yank it out of their gardens because they've been told that it is a pest instead of a beautiful flower and a medicinal treasure.

The river has shifted a little since last year, but the swimming hole is still there. In seconds, I've stripped off my clothes and jumped in to splash and play. I swim up to the moss and fern-covered embankments to examine them carefully, sure that I must have lived a previous life as a fairy, or water sprite.

Pleasantly exhausted, here I sit at day's end like a big seal, water dripping off of my naked body, warming in the sun. I am home once more, home in the arms of Gaia. I sit and give thanks for the blessing that is my life. I give thanks that there are still pristine tracks of nature where a fifty-something woman can throw off all her clothes and dive into an icy cold river without feeling self-conscious, but instead feel exhilarated and free. I give thanks that I've made the conscious choice to live my life freely and not be tied to what society sometimes programs us to believe is success. I give thanks that I am healthy and alive and that I recognize beauty in simple things.

If we create our realities, as I believe we do, then I believe we can also create the way we pass from this life into the next. When my time comes, I know I will eagerly strip off my old body, step into an icy mountain stream and float face up as I did today, ears submerged so I hear only silence or an angelic chorus, eyes wide open so I can see the glorious heavens above me, and travel gently to a new shore and new adventures.

Raspberries

When you find a golden memory, savor it.
Dr. Barbara Becker Holstein, *Life, the Greatest Ride of All*

As I put the second bite of raspberry pancake in my mouth, I smile and think of how only a couple of days earlier, while shopping at a local grocery store chain in Rhode Island, I had picked up a tiny box of raspberries. I had looked at the price and put it back down, telling myself that I'd treat myself to raspberries next week.

Now, here I am with all the succulent, organic red raspberries that I can eat. Did I create this opportunity to housesit for organic gardeners in New Hampshire? Is it only a coincidence? I only know it is magic that I am here and whether I created it or some other force is at play, I am exceedingly happy and grateful.

I arose with the sun, even before Anton, and took a basket out to the garden to pick only the ripest raspberries, already dried by the sun's first rays. Back in the house, I mixed flour, eggs, baking powder, salt and melted butter like my mother had taught me so many years before, and then gently mixed in the big round globes of rosy red. The old iron skillet was hot and the butter just starting to brown when I ladled in a big scoop, flattened it and turned down the heat.

This action brought back a memory of my mother, standing before the gas stove in our cottage on an island in Maine where my sister and I had spent many happy summers. We made raspberry pancakes with the wild raspberries that we had painstakingly picked.

I took it for granted as a child, but now appreciate the sacrifices that my parents made to give us those opportunities to run wild for the summer. My dad would drive us up to Port Clyde, Maine, load the old boat, and run us three miles out to the uninhabited island where we would spend the summer. He'd stay for the weekend and then return back to the mainland for the long drive back to Massachusetts and his work, returning for a weekend now and then.

I can see that I get my adventuresome spirit from my mother, who bravely stayed alone on an island with her two young children in the middle of the Atlantic ocean with no phone or emergency services. Flagging down a lobsterman was the only hope of getting help. It only happened once . . . but that is another story.

Back to the raspberries . . .

I make coffee, pour real maple syrup on my beautiful pancake, and carry it out to the back porch where I sit in an old rocking chair in the sun. I take the first bite, eyes closed, and savor everything. The delicious pancake, the humming of bees in the fragrant field of milkweed, the sound of the river across the field and the breeze rustling the leaves of the birch trees. Could I ever wish for anything more?

For me, this is heaven. I simply sit and savor the moment, not worrying my mind about how to make money to buy my own cabin in the woods. In this moment, this is my place and this moment is all that exists. I share it willingly with the birds and butterflies—and the tiny bee that has come to the edge of my plate to taste the sweet maple syrup.

He reminds me that to experience the sweetness of life, I need to stay completely in the moment, and to remember that I will always find sweetness if I take the time to appreciate what is right in front of me.

A Fairy Feast

When I sound the fairy call,
Gather here in silent meeting,
Chin to knee on the orchard wall,
Cooled with dew and cherries eating.
Merry, merry, Take a cherry
Mine are sounder, Mine are rounder
Mine are sweeter, For the eater
When the dews fall. And you'll be fairies all.
Robert Graves, "Cherry-Time," *Fairies and Fusiliers*, 1918

This evening, I shall prepare a fairy feast of succulent raspberries filled with sugar. This treat is sure to entice fairies to show themselves. I know they are already there in the garden of foxglove, lady's mantle, and primrose.

I took photos last night, but they didn't show themselves. Perhaps they are unsure of Anton, who prowls the screened-in porch above the garden. I've set the sugary treats on a tiny, beautiful blue glass plate placed in the garden and have called them with my songs. Later when the full moon shows itself over the mountains, I will go once again to join the party.

In the meantime, I have put Celtic music on the CD player. Here on the back porch, I sit with the trees, which are enjoying it as much as I am. The big, old white pine at the edge of the shed says he's glad to hear something other than bird songs. Birds in these trees refrain

from singing while they listen, too. I watch the birches at the edge of
the field bend forward to listen. Beyond them, birds in the woods are
oblivious to what is taking place up by the cabin; they sing and call
their evening good-nights. I feel excitement and sense magic in the air.
What it will be, I'll have to wait and see.

A clap of thunder echoes off the mountains and now there's a
downpour. The raspberry treat has turned into raspberry soup. There
will be no full-moon and no fairies tonight, but what a delightful time
I had planning the party and making preparations.

Many would say I have too much time on my hands. I would just
laugh at them with the knowledge that in feeding my soul this way, I
am far happier than they may ever be.

Crows in My Sleep

I hear faintly the cawing of a crow . . .
It is not merely crow calling to crow for it speaks to me too. I am part of
one great creature with him . . .
Henry David Thoreau

I've gone to the river, picked raspberries and peas from the garden, and now, feeling that wonderful sleepy feeling that always comes over me the second day in the woods, I decide to lie out in the sun and take a little nap.

As I dose I hear the bluebirds playing around their tiny houses in the milkweed field. I swat at a pesky fly that buzzes next to my ear and think how peaceful it is to lie here on this blanket spread on a thick green lawn that I didn't have to mow. There are advantages to not owning your own little piece of paradise and, instead, sharing someone else's.

I hear a crow across the field calling, and then another. I question if they're wondering where I am. I know it sounds strange, but crows and ravens have a way of finding me whenever I'm relaxing or meditating outside. They usually mean an adventure is up ahead. I wonder what it is as I sit up.

I watch one crow fly out of the woods and across the field to the tall pine at the edge of the mowed lawn. Then another lands on the clothesline three feet away from me. Three more follow. Four sit on the old rope while one stands sentinel. I think how crazy this would sound to someone, but I know they are there to rouse me from my reverie and make me follow them.

I try to ignore the crows as they dance back and forth on the line. Their calls turn to whoops that children pretending to be Indians might make. They make me laugh, but I refuse to get up. Ever clever, these feathered creatures fly over the house and I hear them causing a commotion in the garden. Fearing they will make a feast of the raspberries, I gather myself up and run around the corner of the house. There all five of them sit on the bean row cackling in hysterics like a group of school boys, because they've outsmarted me. I throw my hands up in exasperation and they fly away, still whooping about the practical joke they've played.

What lesson can I take from this? Be careful what you ask for? Choose your friends carefully? In any case, laughter is good and some days you have to accept the magic, however it comes.

Sitting on a Back Porch

The great lesson from the mystics is that the sacred is in the ordinary, that it is to be found in one's daily life, in one's backyard.
Abraham Maslow

My back fits perfectly in the old rocker with no seat. A small board partly covers the hole where caning may or may not be someday. It seems adequate and perhaps the owners like it this way.

I feel the first stirring of hunger as I think about yesterday's pancakes. What a blessing to sit on the back porch of this small cabin in a field of wildflowers, home to Lucy and Dexter, artists, musicians, explorers, teachers and keepers of the Earth. Their young charges at the village school have no idea how these two will impact their lives; but I do, and my heart grows warm as I silently thank them for this opportunity to connect to Mother Earth on a deeper level.

Anton, their sweet old cat, is my companion for the week. We rise with dawn and go to bed with the sun. I fill my days working on my book with occasional trips to the river to cool off, while Anton follows the sun around the cabin looking for the best napping place. We're both totally content.

A blue jay calls to me from a stand of birch trees silhouetted against the morning sun, telling me it's going to be another hot one. I agree as I sip my coffee and make the most important decision of the day. Blueberry or raspberry?

Yes, it's easy to feel peace in this idyllic setting. But is it possible to find such peace in a chaotic world? I know it is.

My life has not always had this serenity.

I've endured pain and suffering and hard times as all humans do. Being in nature and turning to Mother Earth for solace and strength has helped me through those difficult times.

I turned to Mother Earth for comfort when my own beautiful mother died and, earlier that year, when my marriage of thirty-three years ended. I called upon God and went to the Earth and was given strength and grace to handle these heartbreaks.

I went to the ocean and meditated on the shore. I found the clarity and courage I needed to make the decision to close my wellness center. I believed it to be my dream. I wanted it so desperately to be my path, but it wasn't. I was being smothered by office duties, and my creativity was being stifled by being confined by a 9-to-9 job. I needed air! And trees and birds and bugs. Yes, there would be sacrifices, but I had learned from studying nature that there is a perfect order to life; if you allow it to flow naturally, you will always have what you need. I spent much time in the woods drawing upon Mother Earth's energy for comfort and support as I struck off into the unknown. It is one of the best decisions I've ever made.

Later that year, I drew on Mother Earth's energy once again to help me support my best friend as she endured a painful cancer and later, her death. Loss is never easy, but I know I was aided in these situations by the strength that I derive in my relationship to God, which presents itself to me in the spirit of nature. When I hug Mother Earth, I feel a hug back from God.

Spending time observing and appreciating nature I have become aware of the natural order of life. Everything has its season and is meant to flow together effortlessly.

I have come to see that birth, life, and death are all miracles. In celebrating the changes, I honor my life and those I've loved.

Making the Connection

Exercises and Meditations to Help You Connect to the Natural World

"I Am The Earth" Meditation

Here is a very enlightening meditation by Joules and Ken Taylor.
I guarantee you will see the world from a totally different perspective
after experiencing it.

Lie quietly, and breathe slowly and deeply for a few minutes, relaxing and clearing your mind.

Imagine yourself as the Earth, a beautiful glowing jewel surrounded by a void.

Imagine your skin as the surface of the planet, your physical features the mountains, rivers, and seas.

Your bones are the rocks that make up the inner structure; your organs, the precious metals and gems deep underground.

The deep-sea currents that keep the planet's temperature steady and capable of supporting life are your bloodstream.

Move slightly, imagining the great tectonic plates shifting against each other. Envision the regulatory systems of your body as the volcanoes, earthquakes and weather systems that release pressure and keep the planet healthy.

Feel yourself perfectly balanced, serene, nurturing and calm—a haven for the various life forms that exist within you.

Then imagine that your body is infested with parasites that bite, claw and foul their way across you leaving destruction behind them. Your attempts to rid yourself of them—by inflicting disease and disaster upon them—are mostly unsuccessful.

All you have is the grim satisfaction that, by damaging you, they are sowing the seeds of their own demise . . .

It's an unpleasant scenario, but a fairly accurate one. Consider what you can do to improve matters.

We all have a responsibility to the planet, if not for ourselves then for future generations. And while one person can rarely make that much of a difference on their own, enough individuals working towards a common goal—even if they aren't aware of each other's existence—make a very big difference indeed. The rewards are immense, in terms of personal satisfaction as well as environmental improvement.

Why not start your own Earth Healing circle as I have. Invite your friends, family, and community to join with you once a month to connect to Mother Earth and hold the energy of peace and compassion for the planet.

Your Guide to Connecting to Spirit Through Nature

I start every day with this beautiful Native American Blessing.

Oh, Great Spirit.

Thank you for this beautiful day.

Thank you for the blessings I have received and for the blessings I am about to receive.

Ah ho.

Now you're ready to make your connection to Nature and Mother Earth.

Exercise 1

A walking meditation is a wonderful way to begin your connection to nature. Most people in our bustling world are in constant motion. To ask you to sit without speaking or moving for more than fifteen minutes in the beginning would most likely present a challenge. I don't want to challenge you; I want to entice you to make your acquaintance with the natural world.

Find a peaceful, safe place in nature where you can walk uninterrupted. Allow yourself enough time so you will not feel rushed. You can go with a friend as long as you remember that this is a silent and individual exercise for each of you.

Before starting your walk take a few deep breaths and stretch. Inhale and relax sending your mind the intent that this walk is for the purpose of connecting to Mother Earth.

As you start to walk along, be conscious of the Earth beneath your feet. Feel how she absorbs your steps. Feel the aliveness of her.

Feel the sun on the top of your head, your shoulders and other places as it strikes your body. On a sunless day what does it feel like? Is it cool or warm? Is it dry, damp or balmy? What does it feel like on your skin and in your hair?

Feel the air circulating around you. Smell the air. Is it sweet, pungent or earthy with decay? Indigenous peoples and those connected to the Earth like myself believe that everything has a spirit. When you walk along with your senses open like this, it is possible for animals, insects, rocks, trees, and plants to communicate with you.

As you walk, become aware of the mineral kingdom. Have you ever been drawn to pick up a particular stone? Stones are the record keepers of the Earth. I use them in my healing practice. You may believe that you are picking up a particular stone because of its color or shape; but actually, you are choosing it because it is sending out energy to draw you to it. It either has a subconscious message or healing property that you need today. If you came upon the same stone on a different day, you most likely would not even see it.

At another time you might have the opportunity to sit among a lot of stones, or on a very large boulder. Ask them at that time to take away any negative energy that you are carrying. They are incredible healers and if asked are very willing to remove depression, anxiety, or pain.

Do you notice any particular plants as you walk along? If so, stop and examine them. Look at the colors and patterns. Feel the texture. Are they rough like the bark on a tree, sharp like the prickers of a thistle, or cool and smooth like moss? Smell them. Experience them and become aware of their aliveness. See how different each individual plant of the same variety can be. Just like people.

Are there animals nearby? What sounds do they make? Take a few minutes to observe them playing, gathering food, or protecting themselves.

This exercise is to help awaken your senses and become aware of the Earth as a living being.

Always acknowledge the beauty you have witnessed and thank them for their gift to you.

When you walk regularly in the same area you will become aware of minute changes . . . a plant has flowered, an animal has been searching for food or shelter, a wind has come through and bent a tree.

Soon you will be seeing and sensing and intuiting more of what is around you. With continued practice, you will start to see the energy that is just beyond our normal field of vision. This will allow you to see the true essence of the land, plants, and spirit guides.

You should do this walking meditation at least three times during the week.

Exercise 2

O Great Spirit, thank you for this beautiful day.

Take a walk into the area where you wish to make your connection. It may be your own backyard or woods, or you may have to drive to a nature center or park. It will be worth it to have a quiet, private place where you will feel safe and not be interrupted.

Feel the sun on your head and shoulders. Feel the air, warm or cold, on your skin. Feel the air moving the hair on your head and touching your face. Is there moisture in the air? Feel your feet upon the Earth as you walk. What do you hear? Open your mouth, breathe deeply and taste the air. Be completely aware of your surroundings with all of your senses.

Find a comfortable place to which you seem to be drawn. Sit upon the Earth, a rock, tree, or stone wall. Gaze at your surroundings with soft eyes. Let any thoughts come, and tell yourself you will attend to them later.

After a couple of minutes breathe deeply.

Relax. Start at your feet and relax each part of your body. Be very comfortable. Just relax and breathe. Close your eyes. *Do nothing.*

When thoughts come just let them pass through. *Just sit and be* for 10 minutes. Be aware of the feel of the sun, dampness on your skin, heat, or cold breeze blowing the hair. Listen . . . to nature. Focus on nature and her sounds, not sounds being made by man . . . Just relax and be.

Open your eyes, relax, and thank the Great Spirit and the Earth for this time together. Leave the spot.

Return to the same spot each day, or as often as you can for a week or two, until you feel really comfortable there. If this doesn't feel like a safe, comfortable place, find another. The energy of some places are more inviting than others.

Exercise 3

To be done after a week or so after Exercise 2. Don't rush to do this.

Go to your sacred spot. Do the relaxation exercise.

Now, sitting upon the Earth, stone, or log, completely relax your root chakra, which is your hip and bottom area. Just sit, relax, and be aware of the Earth beneath you. You will start to feel a warmth as the Earth reaches out to connect with you. Imagine now that you are drawing this red, warm energy up and into your body. You feel it flow through all parts of your body, warming and relaxing it.

Next, imagine white light coming down from the universe, down through the top of your head and flowing into your body. The two energies meet at your heart and mix. Imagine pink energy flowing through every cell of your body. When your body is full, let the energy expand out through your pores into the universe. You have now become one with the universal energy. It is in this state that animals, birds and nature spirits will feel comfortable in your presence.

Remain in this state for as long as you like. It will feel quite pleasurable and sometimes is mistaken for sexual energy. It is the life force of the universe that you are feeling.

Thank the Universe and the Earth for their energy.

As you consistently go to your sacred spot to connect to the Earth, you will start to draw her ley lines (energy lines) closer together. She will be creating a powerful energy vortex for you to work in. With a dowsing rod you can keep track of this occurring. This is your own personal power spot. You soon will find that you are hearing messages from Spirit and communicating with the natural world.

When you leave your sacred place and return to the everyday world, you will appear different to others. Don't be surprised if people stop to stare at you and smile. Your inner beauty is now showing on the outside.

Connecting to Nature Indoors

You can connect to the Earth's energy even when you're unable to be outdoors.

1. Find a comfortable spot situated near a window with a view of the outdoors, or an altar you've created from natural objects. Include a photo of a special place in nature: one you have visited where you feel a connection and to which you would like to return, or a place where you have not yet been but to which you feel connected. Gaze out at this natural view or at your altar, paying particular attention to anything that catches your eye.

2. Now, close your eyes and imagine that you are growing a root that will go down through the floor, through the foundation and deep into the center of the Earth. Imagine the energy of Mother Earth being drawn up through the root to where you sit and into your belly. You are now connected to the Earth.

3. See your chosen sacred place in your mind. Use your imagination and experience this place as if you are there now.

4. Feel it. Feel the air. Is it cool or warm? Damp or dry? Is it still or with a breeze?

5. Smell it. What does it smell like? Take in all the different smells.

6. Can you feel the Earth under your feet? Are you barefoot? Is it wet on your feet or dry? Sandy or moist? Are you standing on stones or grass or sand or moss? Feel the texture on your skin.

7. Hear it. Do you hear birds or animals? Do you hear trees or leaves or grass rustling? Do you hear the heartbeat of Mother Earth? What do you hear?

8. Stay there and just be. Experience it and relax and breathe it all in and enjoy the experience as if you are outside in nature. This is your sacred spot to connect with Mother Earth. She will connect to you even inside if you have the intent. Let her send you healing energy and messages.

9. Thank her for giving you this sacred place and any messages she may have given you. You may or may not recognize them, but they have entered your heart.

10. Come back to the present. Keep the peaceful, loving feeling. The next time you get stressed, take a moment and breathe, close your eyes and see your sacred place. It only takes a few seconds. You can leave everyone and everything behind. It is a safe place where no one else can go unless you invite them in.

Connecting to the Earth for Planetary Healing

Close your eyes and imagine that where you sit upon the Earth, you are forming roots like a tree, sending them down through all the layers and deep into the womb of Mother Earth.

You feel the warm embrace of your Earth Mother and embrace her back.

Now, let your roots grow outward meeting and intertwining with other roots of those all over the planet consciously connecting for the same reason of maintaining peace and compassion. Feel the strength and support we give to the planet while connected with intent.

Next, I'd like you to imagine that your roots are thirstily drinking in the warm life giving energy of Mother Earth, drawing it up through all the layers, back to where you sit and into your body. It travels from your seat up into your belly, your power center. From there, you feel its warmth spread through your legs and up into your chest and down your arms. You feel it travel up your back and shoulders and neck and into your head. You allow this energy to travel through your body healing as it goes.

At this time, I want you to imagine that the top of your head is opening and a column of sparkling white energy from the universe travels into this opening and down to your heart. From your heart you feel it travel throughout your body mixing with the Earth's energy. You may see this as pink energy formed from the Earth's red energy and the Heaven's white energy.

Your body may tingle or vibrate or buzz. You allow this energy to completely fill your body and then ooze out through the pores of your skin.

At this point, you are connecting Heaven and Earth and sending that energy out into the world.

As you sit, allowing these mixed energies to combine and flow through you and out into the universe, you will feel yourself become one with all that is as you become pure energy. When practiced and done properly, you will no longer feel your body. Sit as long as you wish in this state of pure bliss.

When ready, close your root chakra. Now, putting your hands upon Mother Earth, send the energy flowing through you from the heavens down into her. Do this for as long as you wish, knowing that you are feeding her and giving her added strength.

Now close your crown chakra and open your eyes.

Do you notice a difference? What you look at may appear new and brilliant. You may be aware of colors and patterns that you have never seen before. Remember you are still full of this energy and will carry love, peace, and compassion with you throughout the day. Everyone you encounter will be blessed with a healing.

I have had profound experiences after doing this meditation. People have been known to stop right in their tracks and break out into wide smiles. The first time it happened, I thought I must have dirt on my face, or a bird's nest in my hair. Nope. What they were seeing was my essence . . . my body really wasn't visible to them. They were experiencing love and peace and the essence of Mother Earth.

Recently while in India, I led a small group of people in this meditation. When we opened our eyes, three street dogs, who never come near people, were sitting in our circle looking at us adoringly. When we left this courtyard of the Dalai Lama's monastery where we had been meditating, groups of people came over, bowing and asking if they could have their pictures taken with us. We have no idea what they were seeing . . . but it must have been a very bright and beautiful energy.

Try it; you'll be amazed and amazing.

September 15, 2009

A Channeled Message from Mother Earth

Ah, my child,

You ask for a message for those who read your book. Tell them I thank them for inspiring you to come to me more often . . . and to listen. It is good.

My message to them today is to learn to *be* with me once again.

You have all become very good at shutting me out. When it is *hot* you close yourself in buildings and breathe recycled air. When it is *cold*, you do the same. When it rains or thunders or the wind blows you do the same. You sit inside and tell each other how *bad* the weather is. You shut yourself away from the elements and my gifts. You think it protects you and makes you feel better, when the reality is that by shutting yourselves away you are not receiving the healing gifts that I offer, and that is what makes you feel heavy, depressed, angry or uneasy.

The heat is to help your body get rid of poisons and to remind you to drink water to flush them out. The sun activates chemical processes in your body that you need to stay strong. Cold weather is to help your body slow down and rest. Rain is to moisten and keep your body supple inside and out. Water is good. I have asked you in the past to pray to water. It needs to be respected. Thunder and wind clean and recharge the air as well as your body's electrical system so that you stay connected to my energy.

Stop fighting me and the elements and relearn how to *be* in all kinds of weather. You will face many extremes of weather in the future, but you will adjust—and the time to start is now.

You complain about the heat. You complain about the cold. Your bodies were made to adjust to the temperature changes as the seasons changed. You complain about birds who wake you too early in the morning, You complain about bugs that are doing a good job of cleaning up after you. You complain about those indestructible plants that someday will feed you once again, calling them weeds. You have forgotten about the natural order of life. It is time to relearn the old ways. Learn from those cultures who have retained the knowledge of how to live with me and not off me.

It's time to stop fighting and accept and be grateful for everything. You will find that when you stop fighting nature and the elements and give thanks for what I give you each day, it will always be tolerable and mostly wonderful. Remember to connect to me often and raise your vibration with thoughts of joy. Share this joy with others and teach them what it means to *be* with me.

I can feel more of you awakening and it pleases me. I thank you for your love and acknowledgment.

Remember: we are One.

Afterword

Walking gently upon the Earth is much more than communing with nature and having mystical and magical experiences.

To truly walk gently upon the Earth is to have as little negative impact upon the natural world as possible. It means to live being conscious of the fact that we must live interdependently with the natural world in order to survive. It means comprehending that without the oxygen given off by green living things and water from lakes, rivers, and water deep within the Earth we could not continue to live on this planet.

To walk gently upon the Earth is to protect our natural resources. It means making choices that will save our forests, waters, insects, animals and birds, choices that are often not always the quickest, easiest and most convenient.

To walk gently upon the Earth means changing from a throw-away society to one of sustainability. It means making simple, thoughtful changes such as choosing reusable mugs and plates instead of disposable.

To walk gently upon the Earth means caring as much for future generations as we do for ourselves.

We are living in a time of great change. Prophesies of the Mayan and Hopi and other indigenous cultures are coming to pass. We would do well to pay attention to their teachings. They share that the Earth is awakening and her vibration is changing. It is important that we raise our vibration along with that of the Earth, so we may stay healthy in body, mind, and spirit. The easiest way to do this is to make an energetic connection with her.

I believe we have each come here with a mission to do, which will help move the planet forward. The Earth has many energies available to help make this transition one of peace and light. The consciousness of the Earth which is developing and pulsating at a higher rate will help our own awakening. When we learn to align our own energy with that of the Earth's, we will move forward effortlessly.

When we slow down and allow our senses to open, great transformations occur. Living on the planet Earth becomes living in the Garden of Eden.

My wish is that you have found the contents of this book an inspiration, source of enjoyment, and motivation to connect more fully to the natural world.

An Evening Blessing

Mother/Father God. Oh, Great Spirit

Thank you for this beautiful day.

Thank you for all the blessings I have received

And those I am about to receive.

Ah Ho, Amen

About the Author

Linda Hogan has been called a mystic, a healer, an intuitive, and a teacher.

She, however, calls herself a lover of people and the Earth. She believes her mission is helping others to awaken to the beauty and healing properties of this beautiful planet we live on.

Since a child, Linda has been communicating with Mother Earth and the natural world. Her deep love for the Earth later led her to study with indigenous peoples from many countries. She has studied with shamans and medicine people from North America, Central America and South America, as well as Asia. She feels her greatest teachers have been Mother Earth and her spirit guides. To honor these teachers, she has sat on the boards of many environmental and humanitarian organizations.

Linda is an energy healer and teacher, living in Rhode Island. She also leads small group trips to sacred energy places around the globe.

Contact Information

gaia_healer@yahoo.com
www.sacrednewearth.com
www.naturalwaystowellness.com

Inspirations

- Baldwin, Christina (1991). *Life's Companion: Journal Writing as a Spiritual Quest*. New York: Bantam Books.

  I began my first nature journal after reading this empowering book.

- Cullen, Noreen Palladino (1995). *One Spirit Wrapped in Flesh: A Personal Transformation*. Glastonbury, CT: self-published.

  To find someone else with fairy experiences was a blessing.

- Andrews, Ted (1993). *Animal-Speak: The Spiritual & Magical Powers of Creatures Great & Small*. St. Paul, MN: Llewellyn Publications.

- Andrews, Ted (1993). *Enchantment of the Faerie Realm: Communicate with Nature Spirits & Elementals*. St. Paul, MN: Llewellyn Publications.

  Both are always a resource to help explain my encounters with the natural world and nature spirits.

- Howell, Francesca Ciancimino (2002). *Making Magic with Gaia: Practices to Heal Ourselves and Our Planet*. York Beach, ME: Red Wheel/ Weiser.

  A confirmation of the ceremonies and practices that Gaia was calling me to do.

- Kaza: Stephanie (1993). *The Attentive Heart: Conversations with Trees.* Boston: Shambhala Publications.

  You can only imagine my joy upon finding another who had conversations with trees.

- Comtois, Roland M. (2009). *And Then There Was Heaven: A Journal of Hope and Love.* East Killingly, CT: Chalice Publications.

  Every Earth Keeper needs an Angel Connection to stay in balance.

- Taylor, Joules and Ken (2001). *Clairvoyance: How to Develop Your Psychic Powers.* London, UK: Connections Book Publishing.

  "Make Yourself at Home" meditation: I was so pleased to be given permission to use this beautiful meditation in my own book. Everyone in the world should experience what it feels like to be Mother Earth.

- Tam, Tom (1996). *For The Love of Nature.*

  Master Tam is a loving and compassionate healer and teacher. To be in his presence is an uplifting journey.

His Holiness the Karmapa, who blessed my work with the Earth.

His Holiness the Dalai Lama, whose beautiful energy radiates Heaven on Earth.

Grandfather Alejandro Cirilo Perez Oxlaj, Keeper of the Mayan Prophecies. Dear tata, thank you for your wisdom and for striving for peace among all peoples and the Earth.

My wisdom teachers, Bernardo Peixoto "Ipu" from Brazil and his wife Cleicha from Peru. Shaman Jorge Luis Delgado and Shaman Jose Luis Herrerra from Peru. Tibetan Elder Tashi Choemphel Kangasar who recognized my life's purpose and instructed me in working with the sacred energies of India. My Native American friends, and first Earth teachers, those of you living and those who have traveled the good red road to the end, thank you for sharing with me.

My sister authors and the Shining Stars in my life, Gilda Arruda, Pat Hastings and Linda Pestana, whose own stories and journeys are an inspiration. Thank you for taking me under your beautiful angel wings and bringing out the best in me.

Sources

Following are the sources for the quotations I include at the beginning of many of my chapters.

Websites

- www.gaia.com: The quotations by Martha Graham, Cheryl Batoon, Abraham Maslow and Japanese proverb.

- www.brainyquotes.com: The quotations by Thich Nhat Hanh, Mary Catherine Bateson, John Muir, and Theodore Roethke.

- www.naturequotes.com: The quotations by Henry David Thoreau and Rachel Carson.

- www.allgreatquotes.com: The quotations of James M. Barrie, Robert Graves, and William Shakespeare

- www.bellaonline.com: A quotation by John Muir.

- www.Beliefnet.com: The quotations by Ann Ruth Schabader and Hafiz.

- www.ashiraasks.blogspot.com: The quotation by Rev. Ashira Goddard., with permission

- www.thegardendigest.com: The quotation by David N. Elkins

- www.globalstewards.org: The quotation by Saraha

- www.islandnet.com: Japanese Haiku Poem by Basho

- www.thequotationspage.com: The quotation by Albert Einstein

- www.proverbia.net: The quotation by Epictetus

- www.enchantedself.com: The quotation by Dr. Barbara Becker Holstein

Books

- Stamps, Laura (1996). *Songs of Power*. Columbia: Emmanel Publishing.

- Roberts, Elizabeth and Elias Amidon, editors (1991). *Earth Prayers*. New York: Harper Collins.

- Comtois, Roland M. (2009). *And Then There Was Heaven*. East Killingly: Chalice Communications.

- Finneran, Richard J., editor (1997). *The Yeats Reader: A Portable Compendium of Poetry, Drama and Prose*. New York: Scribner Poetry.